Ladies'
Pages

African American
Women's Magazines
and the Culture
That Made Them

Noliwe M. Rooks

Rutgers University Press

New Brunswick, New Jersey, and London

Library of Congress Cataloging-in-Publication Data

Rooks, Noliwe M., 1963–
    Ladies' pages : African American women's magazines and the culture that made them /
Noliwe M. Rooks.
        p.   cm.
    ISBN 0–8135–3424–0 (alk. paper) — ISBN 0–8135–3425–9 (pbk. : alk. paper)
    1. African American periodicals—History—20th century.   2. Women's periodicals,
American—History—20th century.   3. African American periodicals—History—19th
century.   4. Women's periodicals, American—History—19th century.   I. Title.
PN4882.5 .R66 2004
051'.082—dc22

                                                                        2003018868

British Cataloging-in-Publication information for this book is available from the British Library.

Manufactured in the United States of America

For Bill,
who
taught
me to
believe

Contents

Illustrations

Acknowledgments

THERE are a number of stages in the process of first thinking about, then writing, rewriting, and finishing a manuscript. While going through it, I tend to believe each individual stage will be the most difficult. The fact is, they all present challenges and none could be completed without significant assistance. I have had both professional and personal support at each stage. In some ways, it is difficult to separate the two categories.

Soon after I first knew I wanted to write something book length about African American women's magazines, Nell Irvin Painter sent me an unexpected e-mail asking what I was working on. I replied to say I had the beginnings of an idea. She replied asking if I would like a postdoctoral fellowship. Since that time almost six years ago, Nell has remained a constant source of support. From reading drafts of chapters for this book and offering advice ranging from "This is important" to "Let this idea go," from addressing my rants about perceived slights with a sure-voiced "Forget about them"(though her language was a bit more colorful) to commiserating about the state of the world, she has never failed to listen, respond, be present. Professionally, her help has been invaluable. Personally, her presence is a balm.

In 1997 I met Claudia Tate. A few years later she was diagnosed with cancer and passed in the summer of 2002. During that time, she responded to my professional frustrations, bouts of writer's block, and doubts about this project in the same way. She would sigh, say something about how she knew whatever it was must be very difficult, then conclude, "Just do your work." During the last year of her life, she asked if I would give her pages of this book to read and critique. During the last few months, she never failed to ask how it was going. When I wrote the last sentence of the last chapter, I answered aloud to the voice that now resides permanently in my head, "This work is done."

A few years ago, Valerie Smith and I had a standing date to walk five miles twice a week. When we would first lay eyes on each other on those mornings, she would always ask, "How are you?" I came to understand that the question was an honest one. She wanted a real response. We walked in the snow, rain, dark, and cold. We talked about work, relationships, writing, and ideas. I always knew that the days we walked would be very good days for writing. The miles taught me the benefit of balancing the personal and professional. Valerie showed me the value of privileging emotional, mental, and physical health above all else.

There have been groups of readers and listeners at the Schomburg Center for Research in Black Culture, Princeton University, the University of Maryland–College Park, and the University of Delaware who have all taken the time to offer feedback, correction, cogent questioning, and critique. Tim Watson, Marie Griffith, and Grace Hong all stand out in this regard. They made it far less scary to share work that is not perfect or finished and gave me gifts of insight, understanding, and connection that fortified me and strengthened the manuscript.

At Rutgers University Press, Leslie Mitchner patiently waited year after year for a finished manuscript. Every six months I would get an e-mail gently asking how things were going and how much more time I would need. Despite the fact that she never pushed or complained, I began to dread the thought of telling her yet again that I needed another semester, month, or week. Her e-mails made it clear that getting the manuscript mattered to her. As a result, it mattered a bit more to me too.

Only I have read the pages of this manuscript more times than has my husband, Bill Gaskins. Only I have worried about it actually getting finished more than has my son, Jelani Cherryrooks. Bill never doubted that those nights and weekends in the library and endless conversations about the long dead would lead to a book others would read. He simply willed it to be true. He simply did everything in his power to make it so. However, it took me a few years to figure out that Jelani had serious doubts that I would finish this book. I began to understand this was true about the time he took to demanding monthly updates and started to wonder aloud why it was he had to get his homework done on time when I seemed to be taking my sweet time with mine. While writing this book is an accomplishment about which I am quite proud, it is the two of you who are the blessing that makes my soul whole.

Ladies' Pages

1

Scattered Pages

Magazines, Sex, and the Culture of Migration

Half-Century was not an impressive publication. But it stands
among those general-purpose magazines that reflected and guided,
to some extent, the newly developing ethos of black Americans
caught up in the drama of the new century, the world war, and
migration from the South into the industrial, urban Midwest.

—*Walter Daniel*

SOMEONE once told me this book is really a detective story, or
maybe even a mystery. This is how I know I have told one too
many tales about my efforts to track down the publications that
form the basis for this project. I do not think they were suggesting
there are holes in the narrative that require them to go sleuthing
for the connections that lead to intellectual clarity. Nor do I
believe they meant this manuscript reads like a mystery. But
because I secretly like thinking about this project in the same way,
I have never asked the person to tell me why they thought as they
did. It has left me free to create my own interpretation.

I think of this book as a mystery not because there is a who-
dunit embedded in the analysis and discussion of the magazines
written about here, nor because I still make the connection
between the thrill of a good mystery's unfolding and the warm
chill I felt when I first laid hands and eyes on the magazines for
which I had searched for so many years. No, I like to think of this
book as a mystery because, since I was in middle school and

discovered Edgar Allan Poe, mysteries have been one of my favorite genres. For a very long time now, I have loved the ways minor characters, hard-won moments of insight, seemingly unimportant interactions, and clues hidden in plain sight so often form the answers to larger questions I did not know I should be asking. I like to think of this book in the same way.

I like to think that using African American migration as a context within which concerns, issues, and narrative strategies from previous eras and geographical areas interacted with and were transformed by the experience of urbanization with its attendant emphasis on consumerism helps to make connections between magazines published and edited by and aimed at African American women during the sixty-year period discussed here. I like to think that "finding" writers, editors, readers, publications, and subjects that have been "lost" answers unasked questions, connects that which was formerly detached, and uncovers secrets hidden in the reading matter of little-known African American women. I think that exploring strategies to combat the cultural constructions of African American women as hypersexual is a narrative thread that, once tugged, unravels previously unknown motivations for many of the readers, writers, and publications discussed in this book. I think about this book within the context of the mystery genre because I fundamentally believe that much of the popular history of African American women remains a mystery. For me, the path that leads to a mystery's center is usually a road worth traveling.

My interest in finding magazines published by and for African American women began with another project. While conducting research in the Madam C. J. Walker Archives for a book on the politics of hair in African American communities, I came across mention of a publication entitled *Woman's Voice*. The magazine was initiated and sustained by African American hairdressers in Philadelphia, and Madam C. J. Walker's company underwrote its expenses.[1] Though *Woman's Voice* was published for fifteen years, initially I could find no copies of the publication or, indeed, mention of its existence outside of the Walker Archives. None of the bibliographies generally counted on to list periodical holdings by research libraries mentioned it. No one on the staff at the Library of Congress had ever heard of it, nor could the staff find any citations for it in their holdings. None of the scholarly works covering the African American press and its history in the United States noted its existence. No newspapers or periodicals published in Philadelphia or on the East Coast reviewed it. In desperation, I began calling African American colleges to beg reference librarians to look in their uncatalogued holdings. After a number of unsuccessful calls, a woman at Fisk University's library finally took pity on me. She sent a work-study student to search in "the one place I can get to easily. Though I have to tell you, if it's not there, I don't think I will be able to help you." Because the universe is benevolent, and the student was diligent, that "one place" yielded two full years of the publication. Having solved the mystery of that publication, I began to look for others. Few were easy to find.

I will save you the details of my search except to say that when African American women's magazines from the nineteenth century through the 1950s are mentioned, it is rare to find a list of libraries in possession of the materials. One is more likely to find, as the opening epigram illustrates, notes or asides saying that the magazines themselves are either lost, missing, or of such minor importance that their absence is negligible.[2] Though absent from most histories of American, African American, and women's publishing, African American women's magazines are far from negligible. They allowed African American women to find work as journalists, printers, writers, and editors; to define personal, as well as group, identities; to create a sense of unity by establishing a communication network among women in different regions; to present and comment about world and local events from an African American female perspective; and to highlight achievement often overlooked and ignored by the dominant or African American male press.[3] While a majority of African American women's magazines published before *Essence*'s appearance in May 1970 are largely unknown, they have existed in the United States for well over one hundred years.

Between 1891 and 1950 there were eight African American women's magazines published for a variety of audiences and purposes. Some, like *Ringwood's Afro-American Journal of Fashion* (1891–1894), *Woman's Era* (1894–1897), and *The Sepia Socialite* (1936–1938) saw their role as providing a space for what one scholar has termed "culture by association."[4] By subscribing to such periodicals, readers who either considered themselves to be educated and refined or wished to be in the future could, despite geographical distance, mingle with like-minded individuals. Other publications, like *Half-Century Magazine for the Colored Home and Homemaker* (1916–1925), *Woman's Voice* (1912–1927), and the Home Magazine in *Tan Confessions* (1950–1952), described themselves as preparing African American women for a place in urban social landscapes and overwhelmingly focused on the significance of consumerism for African American women in those locales. Still others, like *Our Women and Children* (1888–1891) and *Aframerican Woman's Journal* (1935–1954), attempted to speak to specific political, domestic, or religious aspirations on the part of an African American female readership. Of the hundreds of magazines started in the United States between 1890 and 1950, only the handful just mentioned (and perhaps another handful for which I do not yet know I should be looking) could boast ownership and editorial control by African American women.

It is not merely because they are rare that these magazines are important. Their importance lies in their asking us to think more deeply about or, in some instances, rethink what we are sure we know about relationships between groups of African Americans in different regions, and to listen in on intraracial conversations from a number of historical periods and geographic locales. Beyond an opportunity for historical eavesdropping, the ways in which popular African American women's magazines contextualized, portrayed, and communicated societal expectations to an African American female reading audience remind us that mass-produced women's magazines often offer "representations of women which are either downright reactionary, or at least subtly maintain sexual difference and women's subordination."[5] Because I am interested in that which is messy, complicated, and complex within the popular history of African American women, the mechanics of how sexual difference is maintained and subordination perpetuated is at the heart of this book. To shine as bright a light as possible on such areas, I discuss the magazines in an interdisciplinary, comparative framework and in relation to specific themes.

The changing constructs of femininity and gender within the contexts of African American migration, urbanization, and consumerism, along with an exploration of narrative strategies aimed at either confronting or controlling cultural constructions of African Americans in relation to sex and sexuality, form the twin thematic lights guiding the exploration of the magazines discussed in this book. The contexts of migration, urbanization and consumerism are foregrounded because each of the publications attempted to educate a migrant population about the requirements and expectations for societal acceptance in an unfamiliar urban area and used this rationale to explain its existence. What African American women wore, bought, read, cooked, ate, and did at home with their families were all fair game, and each magazine offered copious advice and analysis about what such choices could and did mean. A confrontation of narratives emphasizing African American women's hypersexuality is a focus because it is a topic to which the writers of the magazines repeatedly turned. While they would do so in an effort to refute and at times rework the cultural understandings of such narratives, how the writers and editors of these magazines represent, image, and portray certain groups of African American women in relation to sexuality often bears a striking resemblance to that which they claim to challenge.

In an effort to trace the popular deployment of intraracial narratives that link migration, urbanization, consumerism, and discourses around sexuality to broadly defined strategies for racial advancement, I have chosen to focus on magazines written, edited, published, and primarily owned and read by African American women.

Accordingly, this book deals with publications supported through subscriptions and newsstand purchases, as opposed to those subsidized by political or religious organizations. It primarily discusses three publications: *Ringwood's Afro-American Journal of Fashion, Half-Century Magazine for the Colored Home and Homemaker,* and *Tan Confessions.* Those three magazines cover six decades of publishing history. Each was read widely and subscribed to nationwide. Each was centered in a city that would become a magnet for African American migration, urbanization, business, and consumerism during different periods. Thus, each allows for a focus on African American women's relationship to a culture of migration during a different phase and in all its complexity. It is worth noting that despite my efforts to cast as democratic a net as possible through a focus on magazines that attempt to cultivate and speak to a popular, nonelite African American female readership, in many ways, the ideologies and political concerns of an African American intellectual, social, and political elite nonetheless dictated the publications' editorial content. Such a circumstance is not altogether disconnected from the history of the African American press in general.

THE AFRICAN AMERICAN PRESS IN HISTORICAL CONTEXT

By choosing to narrow my focus to a particular segment of the African American press, I in no way seek to understate the overall historical significance of that institution within African American history. The African American press has represented a diverse spectrum of opinion for nearly 150 years. Between 1865 and 1889 alone, more than five hundred African American newspapers began publication.[6] The explosion of African American newspapers after the Civil War resulted from increases in African American literacy and mobility combined with a need for advocacy in the battle against segregation, disfranchisement, and lynching.[7] As a result, overwhelmingly, African American newspapers from that period functioned as organs of protest. As the century ended, there was a conservative shift within the nation at large and outright protest had to be disguised. The number of newspapers shrank. However, as the number of African American newspapers declined, magazines, often organized to focus on stories and individuals that exemplified racial progress, success, and advancement, thrived.

Although much of the editorial content of African American magazines, with their focus on the social hardships faced by African Americans mediated by representations of elite groups of exceptional leaders and intellectuals, differed sharply from that of general magazines in the nineteenth century, African American publishers did look to mainstream U.S. magazines as prototypes. *The Anglo-African* (1859–1861) was modeled after *The Atlantic Monthly*, and *The A.M.E. Church Review* (1884–present) paralleled *Harper's Magazine* in format. The two most popular African American magazines in the first decade of the twentieth century, *The Colored American Magazine* (1900–1909) and *The Voice of the Negro* (1904–1907), imitated the format of the very successful *McClure's Magazine.*[8] Its close resemblance to a popular mainstream magazine may account for *The Colored American Magazine*'s claim to the largest circulation (seventeen thousand) of any African American magazine in the first decade of the twentieth century. *The Voice of the Negro* was a fairly close second with a high of thirteen thousand subscribers.[9] While popular, neither magazine was able to capture a subscription base capable of keeping it afloat for more than a few years. The first African American magazine to both last more than a decade and claim a subscription base of more than 100,000 was the *Crisis.*[10]

Originated by W.E.B. Du Bois in 1910, the *Crisis* was the official publication of the National Association for the Advancement of Colored People (NAACP). Du Bois's first editorial told readers that the magazine would set forth facts and arguments to show the dangers of race prejudice; serve as a newspaper to record important events and movements bearing on interracial relations; review books and press comments; and publish a few appropriate articles.[11] Though early response to the magazine was enthusiastic, some readers complained that the tone was "bitter" and the news "depressing." Du Bois replied that the *Crisis* did not "try to be funny." He wrote that he remembered all too well the "graveyards of ambitious and worthy ventures" in which the *Colored*

American and the *Voice of the Negro* lay and vowed not to allow *Crisis*'s content to be swayed by too much attention to public opinion or subscription numbers. Instead, he put his trust in the membership base of the NAACP, and the fact that the organization would provide the funds necessary to keep the magazine up and running.[12]

Other magazines founded on the *Crisis* model included *Opportunity,* the publication of the National Urban League, which documented literary and artistic accomplishments of the Harlem Renaissance, and A. Philip Randolph and Chandler Owens's *Messenger,* which was underwritten by the Brotherhood of Sleeping Car Porters. While these magazines paralleled early African American newspapers by protesting conditions that negatively impacted African Americans, and by providing a wealth of political commentary, they were also almost wholly dependent on subsidies from the political organizations to which they were connected to stay afloat financially. It is not possible to know how long any would have lasted had they been dependent solely on subscriptions and newsstand purchases to earn their keep. The African American women's magazines discussed in this book did not have such organizational support.

It is clear that in its early years, the African American press was tightly tied to a tradition of political protest and political organizing. The same is true of African American women's periodicals. However, the nature of the protest differed greatly, as did the ways a focus on an African American elite would manifest. For African American women, slavery, sexual abuse, and the defense of their character and morals in the face of dominant, as well as African American male, sentiments formed the nineteenth- and early-twentieth-century political basis for the magazines they published. Elite African American women wished to claim the mantle of ladyhood, and they used magazines to make their case. Before making the argument, however, they first had to do battle with cultural perceptions about them.

Sensationalistic sexual narratives about African American women had circulated freely during the antebellum period and were firmly imbedded in both the African American and white popular cultural imagination until at least the end of the nineteenth century. When *Ringwood's Journal* began publication, repositioning such narratives became an overwhelming concern for that magazine; it would continue to be a theme as late as the 1920s, when *Half-Century Magazine* put similar discussions in the context of African American urbanization and consumerism. Despite both magazines' asking readers to think about subjects as varied as fashion, domesticity, and product consumption within the context of racial progress and turn-of-the-century possibilities for a modern future, the writers and editors of these early publications repeatedly gazed back at an enslaved past to battle stereotypes and cultural constructions of their characters relative to sex, sexuality, and slavery. In the process, they evidenced troubling and constricting ideas about who many of their readers were, and issues of class, color, and generation greatly influenced the futures they envisioned for some African American women.

Indeed, *Ringwood's Journal* and *Half-Century Magazine* are in some ways almost step-by-step illustrations of how elite African American "ladies" believed that other African American women had been damaged by enslavement and its aftereffects. In column after column, one article after the other, the politically and socially active group of African American women who were involved with these magazines urged the acquisition of what they believed to be redemptive skills, demeanor, clothing, behaviors, and attitudes that could denote distance from a debased and embarrassing sexual history and signal an embrace of dominant cultural understandings of womanhood and gentility. Termed a "Politics of Respectability" by Evelyn Brooks Higginbotham, this social movement manifested in the Black women's club movement at the turn of the century as a mindset that made clear, as historian Deborah Gray White has noted, that

the masses of black women did not measure up to middle-class standards. Believing that slavery had left Blacks deficient in moral, social and hygienic values, clubwomen counseled black women to keep themselves and their homes clean, bathe their children regularly, and provide them with music, games, and books to keep them usefully occupied. Women had to stop sitting on stoops and talking and laughing loudly in public. Girls should stick close to home, and boys be kept from wandering. Families had to live within their means, domestic workers had to stop buying clothes they could not afford. Women should choose their husbands more carefully, save money, and buy homes. Alcohol was strictly verboten, and, above all, women had to lead, and teach their daughters to lead, virtuous lives.[13]

Variations on this narrative theme were consistently rewritten, revisioned, and refashioned in African American women's magazines at the turn of the century and beyond. They were a response to the dominant narratives about the bodies, morals, and character of African American women deeply embedded within U.S., as well as African American, culture. Within both the mainstream idea and the African American male response, African American women's bodies had by the late nineteenth century come to function as ground zero for articulating the relationship between sex, race, enslavement, and citizenship in the United States.

SHROUDED IN SEX: WRITING BACK TO HISTORY

While African American women undeniably progressed in the thirty-five-year period between the Emancipation Proclamation and the end of the century, when the first African American women's magazine appeared, they were still in many ways necessarily occupied with and surrounded by degrading narratives and discourses honed and distributed during the antebellum period. In particular, they were very much engaged in a process of distancing their bodies from cultural narratives that made seamless connections between their race and gender and the signification of their status as either hapless rape victim or promiscuous whore. Given that such connections were reified in law, politics, and literature, such distancing was much more easily imagined than accomplished.

If it is possible to fix a particular period in which the relationships between race, gender, and sex began to be tightly drawn in a global context, it could easily be with the impressions of Europeans who first traveled to Africa. Despite a tradition in art of representing women with their breasts bared, the writers of these wildly popular travelogues of the "dark continent" were not accustomed to seeing women walking around in public with their breasts uncovered at all times. Accordingly, many of these white male writers described African women as lewd. Within these stories, fanciful tales of bestiality involving African women and apes were a popular staple and an early means of differentiating the humanity of Europeans from that of Africans.[14] When African women were brought to the American colonies, their dress continued to add to this burgeoning mythology, as enslaved women working in the fields often were given little more than rags with which to cover themselves.[15] By the Victorian age, a period in which the sight of a white "lady's" ankle was considered shocking, a woman with clothing whose rips and tears revealed much of her body simply scandalized. As a result, the image of women of African descent, over time, came to be closely associated with the lewd and oversexed. Such women were viewed as desiring to inflame passion, and that image was firmly entrenched within the Protestant imaginary and, by extension, within the cultural imaginary of the United States as a whole. Because the Protestant ethic taught whites that "temptations of the flesh" should be delayed in favor of accumulating capital, women "who provoked passion were looked down upon and often punished"[16]

By the start of the nineteenth century, enslaved women of African descent functioned as metaphors for the immorality against which white Protestant men were struggling. One of the most prevalent images depicting them was the promiscuous harlot, or jezebel. The other was that of a sexual victim. Despite such images almost negating each other—the one signifying a lack of agency and the other its opposite—they existed simultaneously and would come to constitute the primary images with which African American women writing and speaking during the antebellum period and after would be drawn to engage. The need for such a strategy was exacerbated by the rise in popularity of narratives of enslavement. In that genre, the image of African American women did not fare much better than it did in U.S. society at large.

Slave narratives were a well-known tool of abolitionists in the mid- to late nineteenth century and were one of the main resources for describing the horrors of slavery to a Northern population. Narratives enjoyed wide popularity between 1850 and 1863, and works by Frederick Douglass and William W. Brown far outsold those by the likes of Henry David Thoreau and Nathaniel Hawthorne.[17] So many narratives were written and marketed between 1850 and 1860 that one reviewer complained, "The shelves of the booksellers groan under the weight of Sambo's woes, done up in covers."[18] Although the clear majority of slave narratives were aimed at and supported by the dominant culture, they and their messages were very much a part of African American communities and enjoyed a wide readership there as well. For example, in the early years of William Lloyd Garrison's *Liberator*, the readership was predominantly African American, and "the number of Negro subscribers far outweighed the number of white supporters, so that in 1831, 400 of the newspaper's 450 subscribers were Negro; and even as late as 1834, seventy-five per cent of its more than 2,300 subscribers were Negro."[19] During the 1830s, African Americans founded more than fifty antislavery societies and initiated several antislavery publications. In 1847 Frederick Douglass began printing the *North Star*, which boasted a readership of 4,500, many of whom were African American.[20] Marva Furman has argued that slave narratives functioned as a prototype for the African American novel and points out that many of the fiction writers who published before 1900 were employed as speakers for one or another of the antislavery societies.[21] If true, given the monolithic representation within slave narratives of African American women as sexual victims, African American men were apparently also responsible for further strengthening the connection between African American women and debilitating sexual images.

For example, Wlliam Craft implies that rape, violation, and seduction were inevitable features of life for enslaved African American women: "It is a common practice for gentlemen (if I may call them such), moving in the highest circles of society, to be the fathers of children by their slaves, whom they can and do sell with impunity. . . . Oh! If there is any one thing under the wide canopy of heaven horrible enough to stir a man's soul, and to make his very blood boil, it is the thought of his dear wife, his unprotected sister, or his young and virtuous daughters, struggling to save themselves from falling a prey to such demons!"[22]

As literary critic Frances Foster has pointed out, Craft's comment about the indignities inflicted upon enslaved African American women being enough to make a man's blood boil reminds us that rape and sexual violation were often written about in terms that highlighted men's inability to protect their wives, daughters, and friends from abuse.[23] Henry Bibb claimed it was sexual violence that accounted for slavery's long duration: "The strongest reason why southerners stick with such tenacity to their 'peculiar institution,' is because licentious white men could not carry out their wicked purposes among the defenseless colored population as they do without being exposed and punished by law, if slavery was abolished. Female virtue could not be trampled under foot with impunity, and marriage among the people of color kept in utter obscurity."[24] In a majority of narratives written by African American men, lengthy descriptions of sexual and physical abuse of slave women and girls by white men predominate. Despite the fact that such sexual practices are roundly denounced in the narratives, the overall effect is a monolithic portrayal of African American women as sexual victims. The competing representation is a characterization that is equally damaging. It is of African American women and girls as overtly and willingly promiscuous.

For example, in an interview conducted by the American Freedmen's Inquiry Commission in 1863, Robert Smalls, a former slave, is specifically asked about African American women's sexual practices:

Q. Have not colored women a good deal of sexual passion?

A. Yes, sir.

Q. Are they not carried away by their passion to have intercourse with men?

A. Yes sir; but very few lawful married women are carried
away if their husbands can take care of them.

Q. How is it with young women?

A. They are very wild and run around a great deal.

Q. What proportion of the young women do not have sexual
intercourse before marriage?

A. The majority do, but they do not consider this intercourse
an evil thing. This intercourse is principally with white men
with whom they would rather have intercourse than with
their own color.

Q. Do they do this for money?

A. The majority of the young girls will for money.

Q. At what age do the colored girls begin to have intercourse
with white men?

A. I have known them as young as twelve years.[25]

Mary Helen Washington has found that only slightly less than
12 percent of extant narratives were written by women, and of
that number, the clear majority were written during the early
years of the genre. As a result, most of what we know of enslavement from those who were themselves enslaved has a male face,
and male narrators were in part responsible for perpetuating sexualized images of African American women in the antebellum
period. William Andrews, Beth Doriani, and others have pointed
out that male narrators presented their stories in a way that highlighted the values and character traits most respected by white
men: courage, nobility, rationality, and physical strength. Their
stories also tended to focus on the heroism and individualism of
the author. While male narrators may have presented themselves
in light of dominant male literary traits, they defined slave women
almost exclusively in sexual terms. As a result, within slave narratives and interviews, as well as in the larger cultural imaginary,

victimhood and promiscuity were two of the most prominent narratives inscribed on the bodies of African American women. Given the popularity of such narratives, it is not difficult to understand why African American women were overwhelmingly concerned with addressing their veracity and fashioning a counterrepresentation that showed them in a more culturally acceptable light. Some of them, they would argue, were more than the mythologies surrounding their pasts. Disturbingly, those portrayed as examples of such transcendence were biracial, or often had light skin and white features, or both.

African American women writing in the pages of African American women's magazines at the turn of the century, while attempting to downplay the significance of past associations with rape, victimhood, and violence, were nonetheless unable to leave the period and its significance behind entirely. Instead, they compulsively attempted to refashion it to signify a period in which at least some of them were able, due to the meaning they fashioned of their light skin and white features, to thrive. Accordingly, sex, sexuality, and combating cultural narratives surrounding African American women and slavery would form the ideological basis for much of African American women's periodical production at the end of the nineteenth century. By the first few decades of the twentieth, narratives centering on African American migration, urbanization, and consumerism would become intertwined with those of the earlier period.

At the turn of the century, and a generation after slavery's end, narrative concerns with promiscuity, rape, and enslavement in African American women's magazines would not be left behind. They would, however, be reworked. Moving to an urban area and consuming the appropriate products came to be viewed, within the context of what the magazines argued was an outmoded representational and narrative backdrop, as a means to shape a new, modern, and libratory meaning for Blackness in general and African American womanhood in particular. In African American women's magazines, that new meaning was tied to how poor and working-class women dressed, acted, and spoke in the public spaces of urban America, and the covers of the magazines written by and aimed at other African American women were offered as examples that had best be followed if such women hoped to ever improve their condition. Indeed, migration and urbanization would heighten the issue of representation for all African Americans.

THE CULT OF REPRESENTATION: "NEW NEGRO" LADIES

With the exception of the Middle Passage, movement has often meant freedom for African Americans. Whether the movement was away from Southern plantations and to a Northern border, or from that same plantation to the woods for time alone, to own one's motion, to choose a destination, meant freedom. When the Emancipation Proclamation was enacted in 1863, less than 8 percent of African Americans lived in the Northeast or Midwest; in 1900 approximately 90 percent of all African Americans still resided in the South.[26] By the early decades of the twentieth century, the mobility of African Americans increased tremendously, and urbanization and migration followed. The significance of migration in relation to changes in African American culture generally should not be underestimated. Between 1900 and 1930, the African American population in urban areas increased by more than three million. Chicago's African American population increased 530 percent between 1910 and 1930; there was a 357 percent increase during the same period in New York City and a 260 percent increase in Philadelphia.[27] This demographic shift involved the oftentimes uneasy mingling of Southern and Northern, elite and working-class African Americans and led to the eventual evolution of a new urban African American culture. More than merely denoting an upsurge in the numbers of bodies occupying particular geographic spaces, those numbers represent a distinct space and opportunity for African American visual and cultural intervention and reinvention.

For example, between 1895 and 1925, successful photography studios owned by and catering to African Americans were a ubiquitous feature of the urban landscape. Addison N. Scurlock in Washington, D.C., Morgan and Marvin Smith in New York, and noted Harlem photographer James Van der Zee made some of their best-known portraits of African American inhabitants of the urban North during this period. From images portraying well-groomed African Americans strolling around the streets of Harlem to numerous studio portraits of African American domestics, decorated veterans, and recently migrated sharecroppers wearing the latest in formal attire and posed in idealized domestic scenes complete with modern iceboxes, radios, and expensive trinkets, Van der Zee imaged a distinctly urban people. Given the photographers' practice of retouching evidence of poor health and dental care or old, well-worn clothes, it is clear that he was, as one scholar has noted, "tireless in devising ways to use composition, image manipulation, props, and stage studio setups to establish a space in which his subjects could expand spiritually, emotionally, and symbolically."[28]

Those who sat for portraits could almost literally invent themselves and their surroundings. The resulting photographs offered African Americans proof that they could fashion an image and, by extension, portray a life markedly different from that represented in mainstream popular culture and in the white imagination. According to Deborah Willis, such photographs are "of a people in the process of transformation and a culture in transition."[29] She goes on to suggest that at the turn of the twentieth century, visual images such as photographs were part of a larger concern with transforming and reinventing African American cultural identity.

As Daphne Brooks has argued, African American migration and urbanization led to a heightened rhetoric of "newness" that held a particular resonance for artists, journalists, and political leaders intent on displacing the distorted, minstrel-inspired images of African Americans that persisted in mainstream popular culture. She further notes that this new image came to be described as the "New Negro," and African American cultural workers called on the figure to displace the "Sambo" and "Mammy" images that continued to occupy more than their share of space in the U.S. cultural imagination and in the editorial content and advertising imagery of mainstream periodicals like the *Ladies' Home Journal* and the *Atlantic Monthly.*[30] It is then not surprising that the popularity of photographic portraits parallels the era Henry Louis Gates Jr. has labeled "the crux of the period of Black image reconstruction." He adds that "almost as soon as Blacks could write, it seems, they set out to redefine—against already received racist stereotypes—who and what a Black person was, and how unlike the racist stereotype the Black original indeed actually could be."[31] Accordingly, the emerging African American communities and urban cultural productions such as magazines formed during and after the turn of the century became arenas in which shifting cultural images were both performed and consumed.

Such dynamics are at the heart of the interactions in *Half-Century Magazine* and *Tan Magazine*. In those magazines, the process of teaching the newly migrated what their social betters thought about and expected from them in relation to the larger political project of creating and maintaining the "New Negro" image would be a major endeavor. *Showing* African American women readers what African American women in urban areas could and should look like was no small part of their undertaking. This was particularly true in relation to gendering images of the "New Negro" and linking the image of "New Negro" ladies with consumerism.

As Lizabeth Cohen has pointed out, at least in relation to Chicago and New York, African American receptivity to mass culture and consumerism was often viewed as a means of participating in what was, for the recently migrated, a new and different urban culture. This receptivity grew in response to increasing calls for a separate African American economy that would combat economic disparity, the paucity of employment options, race-based discrimination, and racist labor practices.[32] The consumption of products for and in the home was argued to be a way of obtaining citizenship rights and societal acceptance within U.S. culture at large. Accordingly, consumerism was viewed as tangible evidence of the efficacy of the "New Negro" image. African American women were the primary targets of these arguments, urged both to consume and to teach the ethos of consumption to their husbands and children. Such views became an all-encompassing narrative in African American women's magazines between 1920 and 1950, where from the covers to the use of African American models to illustrate the stories or advertise products, images of certain kinds of African American women were consistently linked with the ideology of the "New Negro," consumption, and resulting notions of racial progress and advancement.

It is important to note that the cultural delineation of classed, gendered, and regional identities was related to, and yet distinct from, the ways in which magazines aimed at middle-class white women gendered consumption and linked the practice to Progressive Era ideologies of citizenship and social acceptability.

THE NEW WOMAN: CONSUMERISM AND WHITE WOMEN'S MAGAZINES

As Ellen Gruber Garvey has pointed out, at the turn of the century, "middle class" was a fairly recent designation, and "unlike the classes below, the late-nineteenth-century middle class had money to participate in the new kinds of shopping . . . and might . . . for example, have the economic leeway to choose packaged goods over cheaper bulk goods." She goes on to explain that this new middle class was also unlike the classes above it in that "it had a large enough membership to shape mass institutions." Garvey concludes by noting that consumption became a way to actively articulate class position and consolidate definitions of gender by establishing taste markers and then choosing appropriately among them. In short, by the turn of the twentieth century, learning to shop expressed both gender and class position.[33] This development was greatly aided by the overall changes in U.S. publishing.

In 1893 the three large monthly magazines in the United States—*Munsey's, McClure's,* and *Cosmopolitan*—dropped their prices to ten cents, shifted the basis of their enterprise from sales to advertising, and, for the first time, achieved circulations in the hundreds of thousands. Other publications followed suit, and soon magazines in conjunction with advertisers were able to speak to niche markets that included white women readers constructed as and advertised to as if they were middle class, as opposed to elite.[34] Through the increasingly available magazine advertisements, white women were introduced to a burgeoning ethos of class-based consumption that discussed the purchase of advertised goods as the leading indicator of taste, character, and American identity.

Martha Banta has described the mass-produced advertising images of white women that evolved between 1890 and 1910 as the convergence of three distinct female advertising types: the Beautiful Charmer, the New England Woman, and the Outdoors Girl. While the New England and Outdoors constructs tapped into a new awareness of white women as athletic, active, and glowing with health, the construction of the Beautiful Charmer, Banta contends, mediated and threatened to dilute the potentially radical politics of New Woman imagery.[35] By evoking an "apolitical" gracefulness and beauty, the Charmer was designed to appease a middle-class public increasingly threatened by the political and cultural upheaval brought about by the demands of white suffragists and Progressive Era reformers. Unfortunately for those interested in preserving political dissonance, the Charmer was a successful turn-of-the-century image, and advertisers productively used it to both identify and speak to a nineteenth-century white female middle class waiting to be targeted as consumers.

African American women were not portrayed in such mainstream magazines as charming, outdoorsy, or from New England. Mainstream magazines did not speak to African American women at all. In addition, the best-known women's magazines at the turn of the twentieth century were, unlike those geared toward African American women, edited and primarily written by men. In those publications, women were primarily addressed as if the sum total of their interests and activities revolved around the home and raising children. Alternative discourses were few and far between. It was left up to the magazines authored, edited, and read by African American women to inform such women about and include them in the cultural changes afoot in regard to definitions of both gender and class dynamics in relation to migration, urbanization, and consumption. They did so in a manner that grappled with race, injustice, and citizenship in ways never imagined or mentioned in publications aimed toward white women.

THE MIGRATION JOURNALS

The next chapter of this book is about *Ringwood's Journal,* the first popular magazine published in the United States by and for African American women. It tells of a group of turn-of-the-century African American women, details a cultural history of the magazine they created, and analyzes the historical links their stories forge between silence, fashion, rape, and generational memory. Primarily a story about what a particular group of biracial writers for and editors of the magazine perceived to be the redemptive possibilities of "modern" fashion and adornment for African American women at the end of the nineteenth century, it is also about the historical circumstances that led the owner of, writers for, and editors of a magazine dedicated to homemaking, domesticity, and all things "ladylike" to repeatedly scrape their pens over the barely formed scabs covering the presence of interracial rape in the lives of their mothers and grandmothers during the decades-earlier antebellum period. The desire to tell a morality tale suitable for their time but starring the sexual violence of a past rarely written about by their mothers and grandmothers led that group of African American women to portray their daughters and granddaughters as lazy, promiscuous, and partly responsible for their own oppression and economic exploitation.

Chapter 3 explores the "uplift strategy" of an older, elite group of African American women who used *Ringwood's Journal* to disseminate their views about the meaning of fashion among themselves, as well as to their "less fortunate" sisters. At the end of the nineteenth century, for all women, fashion was discussed as a marker of class status; its function was part of a larger project aimed at refuting charges of African American moral inferiority, as well as distancing African American women from cultural associations with rape and sexual availability. Toward that end, fashion was linked almost exclusively with the bodies of light-skinned African American women with white features. Accordingly, chapter 3 begins with a quote from a letter written by Josephine Bruce, a very fair-skinned member of the National Association of Colored Women's (NACW) executive committee and the widow of Blanche K. Bruce, an African American senator from Mississippi from 1874 to 1880. Writing to Margaret Murray Washington, president of the NACW and wife of Booker T. Washington, Bruce explains that her reason for choosing to pass on the opportunity to attend a high-level political function is that she has brought only a few articles of clothing with her and the other members of the committee will most likely have already seen her in her best finery. As a result, she will stay home.

In a clear indication of the meaning of and focus on fashion for certain classes of politically active African American women during the period, Bruce makes clear that when looking at each other, this group of influential African American women hold both themselves and each other to high standards. The stakes were higher still for those who did not belong to this group. In the magazine, identifiably black African American women were rarely presented as models able to embody and represent the myriad meanings of fashion.

Chapter 4 explores how *Half-Century Magazine* communicated to its twentieth-century reading audience meanings about and understandings of fashion and style. At the same time, it explores how the passage of time and the movement of people into urban areas came to broaden the visual representation of fashionable African American women to include those who were not exceptional. Not just the elite members of "the race," or those with light skin and white features, would be portrayed and imaged as able to employ a fashionable corporeal message. Rather, large-

boned, dark-skinned women were represented as the primary purveyors of fashion's message. One of the key changes heralded by
the advent of *Half-Century Magazine* was the liberal use of
African American models on most of its covers and on the pages
of its fashion section. However, while the question of who was
represented as fashionable in the magazine was answered, the
question of fashion still posed a dilemma. In the twentieth century, fashion itself came to represent a dividing line between groups
of African American women: northern versus southern, rural versus urban, educated versus illiterate, homeowners versus renters,
migrants versus long-term residents.

Chapter 5 shifts the discussion from personal fashion to the
home. If fashion came to represent a means to combat a past with
its undesirable assumptions about African American female morality and virtue, domesticity and its significance became a compass
that directed readers toward a modern future. Generational and
class dynamics played key roles in how meanings of home were
both deployed and understood in African American women's magazines. *Ringwood's Journal* starkly portrays only two domestic
options for newly urbanized, working-class women and girls: an
unattainable idealized domesticity or domestic work. The rhetoric
of this effort berated African American women for letting jobs go
begging because they wanted something for themselves other than
"a life among the pots and pans."[36] In a further shift, by the early
twentieth century, "domesticity" came to be shorthand for "product consumption" in *Half-Century Magazine*.

Chapter 6 compares stories of love, sex, and consumption that
starred African American women in the 1920s in *Half-Century
Magazine* with those from the 1950s in *Tan Confessions*. Both
publications featured stories by and about African American
women, and both focused on their attempts to negotiate competing meanings of love, dating, marriage, and shopping. In addition,
both include extended dialogues about the mechanics of living
in homes in urban areas. While the two magazines offer a valid
comparison, *Tan Confessions* made the discussion of African
American women's sexual desire much more visible than had any

previous publication. Indeed, given the editorial commitment in earlier periods to proving that African American women were moral and chaste to the point of asexuality, the stories in this new publication heralded a sea change in the representation of African American women as sexual beings. In the pages of *Tan Confessions,* African American women were represented as overly urbanized and overwhelmingly unhappy. Readers of this publication were cautioned that only within the confines of committed domesticity would they ever be able to fully enjoy the privileges of product consumption, or to find sexual satisfaction and personal happiness.

Chapter 7 brings the analysis of African American women's magazines up to the present with an exploration of the significance of *Essence* and *O, the Oprah Magazine.* Given the realities of U.S. publishing practices, where ownership of the publications is shared with large white business concerns, that chapter asks whether either magazine, within the context of this book project, could be considered an African American women's magazine.

As a group, these magazines represent source material about the lives, thoughts, and political leanings of African American women. At the same time, the location of the magazines in areas of the United States that often go unremarked in African American publishing history helps to broaden our understanding of African American life and activity in those regions in particular, as well as in the United States in general. I do not contend that generalized constructs of African American women as slaves, migrants, consumers, or housewives provide a meaningful lens through which to understand the everyday lives of every African American woman alive during the sixty-year period covered in this book. But I do believe that how women of a later period would come to re-vision, remember, and contextualize those constructs during different historical periods, in magazines aimed at other African American women, starts us down a road that leads to the heart of what has been a mystery.

2

Refashioning Rape

Ringwood's Afro-American
Journal of Fashion

Slavery continues to haunt. The rituals of domination and submission, the interplay of taboos, especially those involving interracial sexuality, require concentrated scholarly inquiry, not another season of neglect.

—*Catherine Clinton, 1994*

RINGWOOD'S *Journal* was the first popular magazine published in the United States by and for African American women. It was also a late-nineteenth-century attempt to come to terms with the meaning of antebellum rape and its impact on the lives of women who were the offspring of such violence. Though still a child when enslaved, as an adult, the magazine's founder, Julia Ringwood Coston, would repeatedly turn her gaze toward the tangle of her southern family history as she rewrote and represented her heritage and its association with rape in the most positive light possible. While for many nineteenth-century African Americans, light skin and white features would come to be highly prized as markers of class privilege and status, until late into the nineteenth century, light skin and white features on an African American body signified interracial rape in the minds of white nineteenth-century Americans. As a result, the cultural project undertaken in the pages of *Ringwood's Journal* had personal ramifications for those who produced the publication. They were interested in turning on their head the widespread beliefs about their bodies,

1. *Ringwood's Journal*
front page, 1893

and in the magazine they would produce their features were recast as prerequisites for intelligence, leadership ability, and femininity.

While the subject of African American women's rape was often written about in slave narratives authored by men, it was a subject rarely written about by the African American women who experienced it. However, in this particular turn-of-the-century publication, the offspring born of such violence would rewrite the silence surrounding the rape of enslaved African American women in order to forge a historical link between silence, rape, and generational memory. At the same time, their project had ideological consequences for women of differing classes, ages, and geographical areas of the United States.

We do not know how many African American women were raped by owners, masters, and overseers while enslaved. There is no way to conjure a definitive number for the women who, like a fourteen-year-old Celia, were unceremoniously initiated into years of sexual abuse on the side of a road, at the hands of a new owner, mere hours after their purchase and before a first glimpse of their new homes.[1] We do however know that rape, or its consistent possibility, was a feature of life for untold numbers of African American women held as slaves in the United States. We know this is true from the slave narratives written by African American men, many of which mention such abuse as a primary reason for ending enslavement.[2] We know this is true because a precious few African American women whisper the reality in narratives and memoirs. Yet we still have quite a bit to learn about how such a legacy impacted the behaviors, self-concepts, and futures of those who experienced rape. As Catherine Clinton has pointed out: "Because the secondary literature on rape deals so exclusively with the rape of white women and this same overwhelming majority applies to the question of historical literature on rape in the South, Black women are all but invisible."[3] We know even less about how such a legacy manifested itself at the start of the next century in the lives of the children born of such sexual violence.

In exploring the connections the magazine makes between silence, rape, and generational memory, it becomes clear that *Ringwood's Journal* is a tangible result of a process through which African American women, one or two generations removed from slavery, attempted to create a self-conscious culture to grapple with the meaning and place of their childhood histories of enslavement, their generalized association with rape and violence (even if they had not been enslaved), and their place within U.S. culture. This project had significant consequences for how the generation to which they belonged defined femininity and cultural acceptance for African American women who were young, poor, uneducated, and not biracial.

In the magazine, one group of African American women argued that while they, as a result of the advantages gained from their white heritage and light skin color, were capable of ascending to the highest realms of femininity, there was quite a bit of doubt as to such a possibility existing for African American women who did not share their social circumstances. They argued that this "other" group of African American women had been so damaged by a past that included enslavement along with its unhealthy levels of sexuality, at least one more generation would have to pass before there was any hope for their redemption.[4] At times they reinterpret narratives of antebellum rape to craft an uplifting and redemptive meaning of enslavement for themselves; on other occasions, they argue that younger, poorer, darker African American women could not hope to escape the sexual legacies of enslavement. In the process, Ringwood and her cohorts craft epic binary battles between good and evil, past and future, rape and respectability, while associating visibility with femininity, enslavement with modernity, and fashion with rape. The magazine and the narratives within are further proof that in regard to the system of slavery, "the psychic cost to blacks, though paid, was incalculable and enduring."[5]

THE MAGAZINE

Ringwood's Journal began its four-year publication run in 1891. The first popular magazine aimed at an African American female readership, it was also the first fashion magazine for women of African descent. Distributed and read throughout the United States and parts of the Caribbean, it was published in Cleveland, Ohio, by Ringwood, who chose to use her birth name in the magazine's title to ensure that so "frivolous" a venture would not "embarrass" her husband, or damage his social standing.[6] Largely, it is a forgotten enterprise with but a few extant issues. It was, nonetheless, significant.

The magazine—which debuted to immediate nationwide praise—was about sixteen pages long and contained illustrations of the latest Paris fashions, dressmaking patterns, articles on dress reform and health, biographical sketches of prominent African American women, poetry, instructive messages to women and their daughters, and love stories. It was what we might today describe as a combination of *Essence* and *Vogue*. One reader wrote that she was pleased with the new journal, noting that "women of considerable literary ability who were unknown beyond the locality in which they lived should not be encouraged to remain in obscurity."[7] She went on to say that the new venture would make such writers and their works known across the country, if not the world, and that knowledge of their existence would benefit the social and political aims of African Americans at large. It was a time when acknowledgment of and a plan for addressing the social and political realities of African Americans were sorely needed.

When the magazine began publication in 1891, once thriving African American communities were beginning, according to Kenneth Kusmer, James Borchart, and others, to congeal into urban ghettos. Families with children were particularly hard hit by this change, and many children suffered neglect, because both parents were often forced to work outside the home. African American families and communities struggled for lack of day-care centers, kindergartens, and job-training classes. Few such opportunities existed. At the same time, in the post-Reconstruction era, African American political power in the state and federal governments dried up virtually overnight; by 1889 there were widespread calls advocating the repeal of the Fifteenth Amendment, which granted suffrage to African American men.

Within this cultural context, African American women writers, speakers, and activists from around the country began to organize in hopes of providing social services and of raising money to address the needs of African Americans. Between 1892 and 1894, black women's clubs proliferated across the country, and in 1895 the separate clubs joined together to become one national organization. The African American women activists who were a part of this effort believed their work to provide services to, and to uplift the moral character of, the lower classes of African American women was essential for widespread political and social reform and racial progress. In addition, clubwomen argued that their own moral standing was an example the entire race could follow and learn from. Toward that end, the newly formed club movement would adopt the slogan "Lifting as we climb" to summarize their work and efforts. Though not an official organ, the magazine was connected with and informed by the ideology of this newly forming political movement, and many of the women who would go on to be its movers and shakers were associated with *Ringwood's Afro-American Journal of Fashion* in its early days.

Mary Church Terrell, the first president of the National Association of Colored Women, civil rights organizer (she would lead a successful struggle that ended segregation in public eating places in Washington, D.C., in 1953), and women's rights activist, wrote and edited the biographical section of *Ringwood's Journal*. Other departments included "Plain Talk to Our Girls," edited by Susie I. Lankford Shorter (in 1893 a "Plain Talk to Our Boys" column was added); "Art Department," edited by Adina White; and "Literary Department," edited by M. E. Lambert. Victoria Earle Matthews, who in addition to her work in founding the Brooklyn, New York, Black Woman's Club was a social worker and free-lance writer for leading African American newspapers, wrote in May 1892 that she wished "positive and permanent success in establishing the journal."[8] The magazine's publisher and owner must have been impressed with these sentiments, as Matthews appears as an editor in the May–June issue of 1893. In total, the list of editors reads like a Who's Who of the turn-of-the-century Black clubwomen's movement. In addition to Matthews and Terrell, Josephine Simone Yates, a community organizer and close friend of Margaret Murray Washington (who was to become president of the National Association of Colored Women following Mary Church Terrell), was also associated with the journal.

In addition to the publication's furthering the aims of the club-women's movement, merely by choosing to refer to those of African descent as "Afro-American" in the title of the magazine, Ringwood situated it on a particular side of a nineteenth-century debate about the relationship of African Americans to U.S. identity and citizenship. Her choice of terms anticipated that century's political and cultural debates that would involve both the name by which African Americans should be called, and that to which they would most readily answer. At the end of the nineteenth century, the terms accepted by many African Americans were "Negro" and "Colored." While from the sixteenth century on,

"Negro" had been the term of choice to designate an individual belonging to the African race who was distinguished by physical features (hair, nose, skin color), near the end of the nineteenth century, "Colored" as a racial designation began to creep into political and social discourse. Both terms based their definition on pseudoscientific racial physiology. While "Negro" reportedly referred to those with a dark skin color, coarse hair texture, and particular type of nose and lips, as historian Deborah Gray White has suggested, the term "Colored" first came into widespread use and acceptance because it denoted those of African descent who were of mixed race, or at least of a lighter hue, and as a result, not covered by the generally accepted definition of "Negro."[9] However, "Colored" as a racial term was often broadened to include any of African descent. For example, though "Negro" would continue to be used in scientific discourse, "Colored" was used both by the U.S. government on census forms, and by those who considered themselves part of "polite" society during the period.

By the late nineteenth century, a small group charged that its inclusion of "American" made "Afro-American" the more precise, all-inclusive, politically useful, and "modern" term. Those who advocated this nomenclature believed that they were entitled to the name Afro-American as much as the French were to Franco-American, or the English to Anglo-American. Some who supported this position offered a psychological basis for resistance to the term, suggesting that the reason there was so much antipathy toward using "Afro-American" had to do with a desire on the part of some African Americans to linguistically and culturally distance themselves from a connection to the continent of Africa and its perceived history of savagery. Perhaps it was such a sentiment that would lead educator, activist, and founding member of the Black clubwomen's movement Fanny Jackson Coppins to report that she "did not admire the name Afro-American, but preferred colored."[10] Moreover, by 1895 at the founding convention of the National Association of Colored Women's Clubs, journalist, activist, and contributor to the by then defunct *Ringwood's Journal* Victoria Earle Matthews would go to some lengths to persuade the new association to adopt Afro-American in its name. She argued that, "as for the name 'colored,' it means nothing to the Negro race. I am not a colored American, but an Afro-American." She was soundly defeated in the vote.[11]

The combination of subject matter and political celebrity would appear to have been a successful pairing, because by March 1892, Ringwood was deluged with letters and requests for subscriptions and story, column, and article ideas from both men and women around the country.[12] Congratulations were received from readers of the magazine in Texas, Virginia, Pennsylvania, and Indiana and from as far away as Port Au Prince, Haiti, where it was hailed as the first fashion magazine for the colored race to have hit those shores.[13] The periodical sold for a subscription price of $1.25 per year (fifteen cents per issue), and its circulation figures reached a high of four thousand copies per month. In addition to its popularity and political significance, it was also a testament to the life of its founder.

JULIA RINGWOOD COSTON: A LIFE IN CONTEXT

Julia Ringwood Coston, the owner of *Ringwood's Journal*, is not well remembered. No one ever promised not to forget her. No holidays are named in her honor, no stone carvings recall her, no roads bear her name, no buildings pay her homage. There are no books written about who she was and why she did or did not become great. She is an African American woman from the nineteenth century whose name is not Harriet, Sojourner, Anna, or Mary.[14]

Ringwood is both paradigmatic and atypical. While having begun and edited the first popular magazine aimed at and written by African American women is an achievement worthy of praise—by 1893, city directories in a number of cites listed "journalist" as the profession for a handful of African American women who wrote for the magazine—the passage of time has not made it easy to fill in the details that make a life either significant or interesting. As is often true when dipping back into history to

2. Julia Ringwood Coston,
circa 1892

write about the lives of those who are not powerful and do not leave the letters, journals, and autobiographies biographers depend on for their bread and butter, details are often a luxury.[15] That is certainly the case here. Indeed, in many ways, details make Ringwood's life almost trivial within the context of histories and ideologies comfortable with nineteenth-century African American women as slaves, servants, and sexual victims on the one hand, and as middle-class clubwomen and proponents of domesticity and uplift strategies on the other.[16] She is all of these, and in the end it tells us very little about her.

The illustration in figure 2 is the only extant image of Ringwood. She is seated in a formal Victorian pose and exhibiting the then fashionable neckline, brooch, clothing, and indirect gaze that for turn-of-the-century viewers would have signaled her status and understanding of middle-class sensibilities. This is the image that appears on the first page of the magazine. This portrait and two copies of the magazine form the bulk of what we know about her, although some facts relating to her earlier life are both available and relevant. In the few times Julia Ringwood mentions her early history, she tells us she was born on Ringwood's Farm in Virginia. While her mother is never named, Ringwood tells us that she "suffered" and went through periods of hopelessness before they migrated from their southern plantation home to Washington, D.C., following the Civil War.

In Washington, she spent much of her postbellum childhood in school, excelling and enjoying it, if her later remembrances prove accurate.[17] Her later childhood was spent as the family breadwinner; she was forced to drop out of school at the age of thirteen and work as a governess in the home of an army general, once her mother took ill.[18] In 1886, she married W. H. Coston, a noted author and graduate of Wilberforce and Yale Divinity School.[19] They had two children in the next four years, a boy named for her husband and a daughter she named Julia Ringwood. The name Ringwood was clearly important, and the magazine's founder kept it close to her always in many different forms. It is telling that after her marriage, she kept her birth name, when she could have legally acquired the one belonging to her husband.[20]

In an editorial profile to introduce herself to her readers, she describes the name Ringwood as something akin to her legacy: "Beautifully situated in the town of Warrenton, Va., is the 'Ringwood Farm,' so called because of its resemblance to an ancient homestead of the same name in Colchester, England, in fulfillment of a promise made to his young wife by its owner that their home should be called 'Ringwood' if the first-born were a girl."[21] Ringwood would appear to have been named after another Julia Ringwood, her white mistress and part owner who was born thirty years earlier, also on Ringwood's farm.[22]

Perhaps Ringwood had such happy memories of her childhood that to maintain a connection with them she chose to keep and pass on the name Ringwood. Perhaps she and her sister were so close that she kept the name so as to be forever joined with her. Perhaps her father accepted her into the family in such a way that legitimated her keeping the name. Perhaps she chose to keep the name as a rebuke to the owner of her birthplace, a Presbyterian minister who, in a collection of letters published after the war's conclusion, repeatedly referred to those who were enslaved on his plantation as "servants" and "ebonies."[23] Maybe she just plain liked the sound of it. Whatever the reason, Ringwood clung tightly to her birth name.

That she did means we are left with a name, place, and experience of enslavement that she alone is responsible for naming and shaping in the minds of her readers. This she does in a manner that consistently puts that history in the very best light possible. When mentioning her plantation home, she describes it as "beautiful," "heaven," and "serene" and, in so doing, is able to begin the process of separating herself from the horror of enslavement and of crafting an alternative narrative about the place and relationship of biracial African American women to that institution. She is not, her reshaping says to readers, from a nameless plantation, nor is she herself nameless, placeless, or to be defined by external understandings of African American women's relationship to enslavement. At the same time, the lifelong presence of her birthplace in her name must have kept the circumstances of her birth always in the forefront of her mind. Perhaps this is the real reason she clung to it so tightly. She may have wanted to ensure that she would never forget.

Although the institution of slavery was abolished when Ringwood was quite young, the South, enslavement, and the meaning of her biracial heritage (along with the circumstances of her conception) loomed large both in her psyche and on the pages of the magazine she founded. Just as she took her "family" name with her from slavery to freedom, from single to married life, from private person to public personage, she also took her attempts to construct a narrative of that period for African American women as a group as she moved toward founding her magazine. Repeatedly, Ringwood gave as one of her primary reasons for starting the magazine "the cruelty of the treatment of African women in the south who suffered in hopeless endurance" before emancipation, stating that such "cruelty touched this keyboard in eighteen hundred and fifty-six" (probably the year she was conceived). This is as close she ever comes to disclosing her feelings about the circumstances of her birth. However, in her rationale for beginning the magazine, it is particularly noticeable that she confined her concern for women in the South to the period before the Emancipation Proclamation when, as she writes, a "Lincolnic voice spoke and they received the protection of the State."[24] That is to say, Ringwood does not make clear the connections between the circumstances of her conception, African American women's enslavement decades earlier, "hopeless endurance," and her desire to address any of it by beginning a fashion magazine for African American women who lived in the northern and Midwestern United States.

Additionally, because Ringwood makes a point of refusing to name, or even to mention, any unpleasantness associated with her personal experience of enslavement, it is all the more surprising that she would locate the impetus for the magazine during that period. I suggest that we view her choices not just as isolated instances of a peculiar attachment to a name and family, or a striking devotion to omission regarding her lived experience of enslavement, but as a rhetorical strategy motivated by her desire to keep the painful realities of personal trauma private. While she is not willing to offer up details to the public gaze, her rationale for beginning the magazine gives whispered hints of the true story of her early family life and the pain she associates with it before lapsing into silence. However, for Ringwood, silence was a tool, and *Ringwood's Journal* is an example of African American women's shifting use of and relationship to silence as a political strategy.

SITUATING SILENCE: RACE, RAPE, AND MEMORY

In a whispered allusion to her experience of sexual violation while enslaved, Elizabeth Keckley wrote in 1868: "I do not care to dwell upon this subject, for it is fraught with pain. Suffice it to say, that he persecuted me for four years, and I-I became a mother."[25] By 1893, in an effort to discuss the raced and gendered uses of silence in relation to African American women's oppression, Ringwood would tell her readers: "The vibrations of our silent suffering are not ineffective. They touch and communicate. They

awaken interest and kindle sympathies which arouse public consciousness and bind it to pity and revolt against the injustice of
the oppression."[26]

African American women whose first breaths were drawn
while enslaved in the South wrote these two quotes. They both
migrated to Washington, D.C., soon after Lincoln's Emancipation
Proclamation granted them freedom of movement and freedom
from ownership. They both worked as domestic servants for powerful government figures (Keckley in the White House as a seamstress for Mary Todd Lincoln, and Ringwood as a governess for a
general in the Union army). They both put pen to paper in an
effort to recount their pasts for themselves and others, the success
of their present, and the possibilities of both their individual futures
and those of many other African American women. In addition,
they both offer examples and rationales for African American
women's use of silence in the face of past and present violence and
sexual violation. While Keckley covers her years of sexual violation with a single stuttered admission of motherhood and offers
her personal discomfort as the reason for the lack of further detail
and discussion, Ringwood urges readers to believe that silence
itself is a weapon against oppression that will ameliorate suffering. In the almost thirty years separating the writing and publishing of the two quotes, silence as a response to the trauma of the
rape of African American women during slavery and beyond
evolved from an individual choice to a collective strategy believed
to facilitate survival and reform.

Though I cannot know what a nineteenth-century reader may
have thought about Ringwood's ideas, in my own century her
words sadden. The evocation and valorization of the "silent suffering" to which Ringwood refers conjures images of African
American women denying themselves the cleansing release of a
scream in response to the violence of slavery and more generalized
brutality, economic harassment, and degradation associated with
both the Reconstruction and the post-Reconstruction(ed) South,
as well as the North during the same periods of time.[27] While we
know that acts of sexual violation against enslaved women were

legion, there is precious little from their own pens about the psychological and emotional costs incurred and the manner in which the debt owed them could possibly be paid.[28] Ringwood's views on the uses of silence evoke images of African American women who are mute in the face of rapes, beatings, and a multitude of daily humiliations—the ephemera of life for so many born African American, female, or both, on either side of the Mason-Dixon Line. Certainly the magazine that Ringwood conceived, edited, and published does not advocate a full-throated discussion of rape and its possible effects upon its editors, writers, and readers. While we are told by some of the journal's writers that they or their parents were exposed to both sexual and physical violence during the antebellum period, those admissions are concealed behind a defensive shield of modesty, chastity, maternal devotion, and, above all, vigilant silence about a debased past best left unspoken.

More often than not, as Nell Irvin Painter's work on violence and slavery in U.S. culture has shown, violence and sexual abuse coupled with silent suffering equals "soul murder."[29] Such a state of living death describes a breathing corporeal body animated by a soul deadened or murdered by violence and sexual abuse sufficient to "compromise an identity." As Painter explains, those affected cannot always register what they want and what they feel.[30] A being whose soul has been murdered may be depressed and angry and have feelings of low self-esteem. Sexual abuse, emotional deprivation, or physical and mental torture can lead to soul murder. Sexual abuse, emotional deprivation, and physical and mental torture were a reality for untold numbers of African American women who were enslaved. As historian Darlene Clark Hine has pointed out: "Because of the interplay of racial animosity, class tensions, gender role differentiation, and regional economic variations, Black women, as a rule, developed and adhered to a cult of secrecy, a culture of dissemblance, to protect the sanctity of inner aspects of their lives. The dynamics of dissemblance involved creating the appearance of disclosure, or openness about themselves and their feelings, while actually remaining an enigma."[31]

Rereading Ringwood's words with this overlay, I cannot help but wonder if the soul makes a sound when it is murdered. I wonder if her valorization of silence could be an answer in the negative. Her reassurances to readers that the absence of sound is not "ineffective," is in actuality an active "vibration" reaching out in search of "pity" and "compassion" from a faceless public consciousness, replaces sadness with despair and fatigue. I do not believe that pity can negate a murder, that silence can save a soul.

Of course, given the nature of reading, the meanings and associations are mine. The conjured souls for whom I grieve may exist only in my mind; the writer gives us very little that would confirm or deny their existence in hers. Are her references merely general reflections, or prompted by the recall of personal experience? To whom does she refer when she mentions "our" suffering? Is it African American people in general? African American women in particular? Despite her writing specifically about oppression and the need for revolt, it is not possible to know the true subject of Ringwood's analysis. This ambiguity lies at the core of my reaction to the earlier quotes and at the heart of understanding the multilayered, turn-of-the-century historical and cultural project undertaken by *Ringwood's Journal*.

BLACK BODIES IN THE KEY OF WHITE: THE ACCIDENT OF COLOR

Ringwood identified herself as, and was identified by others as, of African descent. However, because of the light skin on what was read as an African American body, she had to negotiate a complicated emotional, psychological, and cultural landscape—a landscape where in one instance, her skin color would have been able to open doors to certain kinds of privileges, and in another, it would have in the nineteenth century signaled either a forced or a consensual sexual act best left unnoticed and unspoken. Not just in relation to this one woman, but also in the context of nineteenth-century culture, the meaning and unsettling nature of what Jennifer Brody has termed the "mulattaroon" was ubiquitous and widely circulated in plays, novels, and photography, to name just a few forms.[32] In that cultural context, light skin on an African American body was often viewed as the proof of an incidence of rape (near the end of the antebellum period, nearly 10 percent of those enslaved were thought to be biracial) and as a primary justification for ending the practice of slavery.

For example, while the child in figure 3 is not Ringwood, it is a biracial enslaved child who, as the caption tells us, has been "Redeemed in Virginia." Young Fannie Virginia Lawrence was imaged on this postcard because Henry Ward Beecher had recently baptized her in Brooklyn at Plymouth Church. She was five years old and had been adopted by a white woman who wished to rescue her from enslavement. Fannie's new mother (we don't know what happened to the woman who bore her) immediately had her photographed in order to stir up sympathy for the abolitionist cause, as well as to raise money for her education. This image is one of a set of postcards circulated in the United States during 1863 and 1864; their use by well-known abolitionists was predicated on the knowledge that "the natural aversion to miscegenation was strong and that, generally, abolitionist sentiment did not reflect an innate sympathy for Blacks but arose because many Blacks had substantial amounts of white blood."[33]

Putting a finer point on such sentiments, one nineteenth-century scientist, Louis Agassiz, came to be well known for his daguerreotypes of nude slaves (he took them in an effort to prove anatomical difference and dispute the theories of evolution put forth by Charles Darwin) and went so far as to suggest that the real reason for the Civil War was the abomination of interracial sex practices of white owners and those they had enslaved. He writes: "I have no doubt in my mind that the sense of abhorrence against slavery which has led to the agitation now culminating in our Civil War, has been chiefly if unconsciously fostered by the recognition of our own type in the offspring of southern gentlemen, moving among us as negros [sic]."[34] The light skin of such offspring subtly alluded to family dynamics like Ringwood's and their resultant proximity to whites came to be discussed as one of the reasons slavery had to be abolished. As Brody has pointed

3. White slave child "Redeemed in Virginia," 1863 (Photographs and Prints Division, Schomburg Center for Research in Black Culture, The New York Public Library, Astor, Lenox, and Tilden Foundations)

out, their presence confounded narratives of purity and its relationship to civilization, so important to the self-image of most nineteenth-century Americans.

In a society that equated color with character and civilization, these children were portrayed as hapless victims unable to take full advantage of their white skin or, perhaps, given the right kind of costuming and setting (like that in the photograph of little Fannie), to escape their association with Blackness and slavery altogether. In the minds of many however, they were the result and embodiment of rape.[35] While in abolitionist discourse, such persons were discussed as a reason for ending the system of slavery due to their signification of sex and rape, in literary works authored by African Americans, they became known and described as "tragic mulattos" who were accepted as neither white nor Black but became outcasts as a result of being both.

If such persons were used to denote the possibility of civilization and to decry the slave system when circulated in the dominant culture, they often came to constitute an upper class in African American communities in the United States. Indeed, the mixed-race house and field slaves, along with biracial free persons, constituted the "old Black elite" after emancipation and through Reconstruction.[36] This first Black elite was defined by its phenotypical, spatial, and cultural proximity to the white upper class.[37] Ringwood was one of those able to turn the circumstances of her birth into an entree to upper-class African American society, and many of the women featured in the magazine's pages share a history of enslaved childhoods and light skin, much like Ringwood and other members of the editorial board. This group of women sought to erase the accepted belief that their skin tone denoted an instance of rape and instead attempted to define it as a prerequisite for elite status. Indeed, it was this very history of rape, resulting in their light skin, they would argue, that accounted for their ability to uplift the African American race as a whole.

In *Ringwood's Journal,* those women crafted narratives that highlighted their acquisition of education and ability to remain chaste. Plantations were described as "beautiful" and "serene." Their mothers' forced sexual relationships with masters, if mentioned at all, were reinscribed as happy family narratives that resulted in light-skin privilege for the offspring; the performance of middle-class identities and sartorial practices would wipe the morality slate clean. In short, rape and violence were refashioned and rewritten, though not forgotten.

For example, the May–June issue of 1893 begins with a biographical sketch by Pilot Buoy about Miss Julia M. Mason. Mason was born in Middleburgh, Loudon County, Virginia, near the beginning of the Civil War. Her mother is described as a "perfect" mulatto of "Caucasian fairness" who was nonetheless a slave and, therefore, "subject to the vicissitudes of bondage." Her

4. Julia Mason article and image, *Ringwood's Journal*, 1893

father is half Native American, half African American, and free. In the description of Mason's experience of enslavement, we are told that she escaped any negative experiences. In fact, much as in the narrative we find in Frederick Douglass's autobiography, she was befriended by a white woman who made a project of teaching her to read and write, despite its being "almost a capital offense in those days to teach Negroes."

After describing Mason's racial heritage in some detail, the article discusses her father's remarriage, his decision to buy her from her owner, the family's move to Washington, D.C., and her successful schooling and rise in the ranks of educational institutions. After listing and describing a number of clubs and institutions of which she is a member (the Colored Women's League and the U.S. Baptist Missionary Society among them), the article goes on: "It is an interesting coincidence that Miss Julia W. Mason and Julia Ringwood Coston were dear and intimate friends in their earlier days and they have spent many pleasant hours of their lives together as schoolmates." While their having been friends might have been a coincidence, the narrative shaping of the histories of the two Julias as it relates to the cultural project of *Ringwood's Journal* is not.

Though these women had childhood histories of enslavement, in a series of biographical sketches, it becomes clear that they were not to be understood as having had a negative or "soul deadening" experience of the institution. Indeed, they assure readers that while enslaved they were exposed to culture, literacy, and ideas about refinement. If any readers still harbor misguided notions about what their light skin and history of enslavement truly means, they should know that, although "born under conditions that would stultify the intellect and deaden the sensibilities of any race," such women are "in the foremost ranks of virtuous, intelligent, cultivated American womanhood."[38] Not only do they tell readers that they have transcended any negative cultural associations between their skin and its implication of sexual violence during the antebellum period, but, significantly, it is that very past that has catapulted them to the forefront of African American womanhood in terms of virtue, intelligence, and cultivation.

ACCOUNTING FOR THE PAST

If we take seriously Darlene Clark Hine's formulation of a culture of dissemblance to which African American women belonged and subscribed, a culture that "created the appearance of openness and disclosure but actually shielded the truth of their inner lives and selves," then we must also take seriously the possibility that the narrative threads in *Ringwood's Journal* are survival strategies hidden in plain view.[39] We can begin to investigate the possibility of this magazine's performing the cultural work of an enslaved woman's text that reaches well into the period of legal freedom. We can begin to view this magazine as a document that refuses to fully erase a history of violence and brutality engendered by the system of racialized slavery, but instead consistently returns again and again to just such a past in order to refashion a variety of narratives that emphasize the possibility of *moral* escape exemplified by an urban experience of freedom. These narrative strategies had relevance well into the closing decades of the nineteenth century. They were meaningful to a group of African American female readers who, located throughout the United States and from a variety of class backgrounds and age groups, had in common their attempt to negotiate urban life and culture in the north and Midwest before the great migrations of the early twentieth century. To be clear, this text is very different from the slave narratives that define the familiar genre that privileges the movement of African Americans from slavery to freedom. Yet the direct experience of and legacy from the trauma engendered by enslavement figures prominently in the magazine. The silences found there mirror the use and structure of those much discussed as an element in the narratives written by African American women during the antebellum period and after.

Beyond its obvious relation to the gender and class politics prominent in the writings and speeches of middle-class African American women in the mid- to late nineteenth century, *Ringwood's Journal*, while rarely directly naming enslavement as its subject, instructs women not only in what it means to be an "acceptable" African American woman in classed and raced terms at the turn of the century, but also in their attempts to reconcile for themselves and each other the association of their bodies with that system's psychologically invasive history of rape. It is in this context that I argue for the relevance of the magazine as a type of enslaved woman's text that through whispered silence engages, repositions, and refashions antebellum narratives of rape—though one that did not appear until well after slavery ended and the children who experienced enslavement had become women with children of their own.

Such views did not bode well for readers of the magazine who were not biracial, had little education, were poor, and often belonged to a different generation. Readers who were dark-skinned and not members of the social elite were told that slavery had not offered them the opportunity to increase their levels of cultivation and refinement. Rather, it had simply damaged them. The starting place for undoing that damage involved listening to the advice of their social betters, working hard in careers as domestics, and wearing appropriately fashionable clothes.

At the turn of the twentieth century, not merely the pages of this magazine but the lives of the elite African American women with backgrounds similar to those of the women who wrote for and edited *Ringwood's Journal* consistently evidenced a concern over the meaning of fashion in their lives. The statements they perceived fashion to make about themselves, as well as about African American women as a group, were of ongoing interest. For instance, the magazine argued that a modern sense of dress was one of the leading indications of moral fortitude; the writers and editors demanded adherence to certain tenets.[40] They told their readers that fashion represented class and that middle-class status represented respect and cultural acceptance. Given that the owner, editors, and writers of the magazine belonged to the group of elite, politically savvy African American women associated with the African American women's club movement, it is not surprising that they placed a high priority on the meaning of fashion and used it as a strategy to accomplish broader aims. They were, after all, interested in nothing less than the uplifting of African Americans as a whole.

3

To Make a Lady Black and Bid Her Sing

Clothes, Class, and Color

I will not be able to attend, I only have one traveling dress with me and I am afraid the others may have seen me in the rest already. One must be prepared for social functions on an occasion like this meeting. . . . Clothes are an important part of a woman after all.

—*Josephine Bruce, 1904*

When we reached her house she winked and said softly as she opened the car door that her only disappointment with younger women like myself was that we never wore hats and gloves. But again, she sighed, she was sure it was because we had never been servants. To Aunt Marie, those of us who never had to "show or prove" that we were real women—ladies—seemed to have "forgotten the art altogether."

—*From* Living in, Living Out

Is it possible to see silence? Can an unspoken history of violence and brutality find a language in the swish of a skirt gently caressing an ankle? For the generation of African American women discussed in the previous chapter, the embrace of fashion as a strategy for combating the cultural assumptions about their supposed lack of character loudly answered yes to these questions.[1] In the glare of a full-length cultural mirror held firmly in place by societal structures, stereotypes, and assumptions, fashion came to represent political strategy, class tension, and a politics of color in African American communities at the end of the nineteenth century. The women responsible for authoring and editing *Ringwood's Afro-American Journal of Fashion* were well aware that at every turn, they would have to "show or prove that we were real women—ladies."[2] The task they set for themselves was making sure other African American women learned this lesson as well.

Ringwood's Journal crafted an "uplift" strategy that related fashion to morality. An older, more "established" group of African American women used the publication to disseminate their views about the meaning of fashion among themselves, as well as to their "less fortunate" sisters. Locked as they were in an effort to negotiate and understand the meaning of freedom and progress within the context of a static relationship and analysis of the roles played by fashion and appearance in the public spaces of political meetings, business functions, and social events attended by the elite, they placed discussions of fashion primarily in the context of a "Politics of Respectability."[3] In *Ringwood's Journal*, such a politics privileged the display of fashion as the public performance of morality in order to combat cultural assertions about African American women's perceived hypersexuality. The magazine offered a platform for the dissemination of ideas connecting race, class, and fashion and spoke to working-class African American women about the importance of their not allowing difficult economic situations to interfere with the pursuit of a fashionable ideal. In general, those of the elite classes took themselves as teachers and models and all other African American women as their students. It is not quite possible to tell how willing were the pupils.

The epigraphs that begin this chapter (while not from the magazine itself) offer two significantly different angles of insight into the ways in which *Ringwood's Journal* understood and discussed fashion in relation to African American women at the turn of the century. The first is from a member of the African American female elite of the type discussed in the previous chapter, and the second is from a woman who migrated from the rural South to Washington, D.C., in 1906 to work as a domestic servant. While of a similar generation, the women were from vastly different backgrounds and their differing understandings of why fashion is important become harmonic counterpoints in related tunes. From both perspectives fashion is used to tell a story the wearer thought most compelling. The subject would be the relationship of African American women to dominant cultural narratives of ladyhood and refinement.

In the first instance, fashion was viewed as an important part of presenting a unified image of wealth, refinement, and membership in an elite class of African American women. Even for a meeting attended only by her peers, fashion's dictates were of primary importance to Josephine Bruce, a clubwoman and activist. In the second quote, fashion was viewed as armor that proved to the outside world (both African American and white) that the wearer, while an African American servant, was still a woman deserving of respect. Fashion could at the same time signal membership in a particular highly influential class of African American womanhood and speak to the possibility of ameliorating the appearance of the debilitating economic and social realities of, as well as cultural understandings about, who African Americans were. In short, at the turn of twentieth century, fashion would come to be about much more than beholding beauty in one's own eye.

Representing Fashion, Fashioning Representation

In *Ringwood's Journal*, "[c]hanges in clothing and in the discourses surrounding clothing indicate shifts in social relationships and tensions between different social groups that present themselves in different ways in public space."[4] The magazine's pictures, articles, obituaries, and biographical sketches turn repeatedly to elite African American women in order to represent their bodies, fashion choices, and characters as models of African American ladyhood, a construct used to suggest that such women presented raced and gendered identities capable of combating negative cultural assumptions about the morality of African American women. But as examples of what was considered most fashion-able, the magazine offered images of white women on its fashion pages and in its advertisements and articles. Identifiably Black African American women were rarely presented as models able to embody and represent fashion. In much the same way that strate-gies of silence in the reconstruction of historical memory operated in the lives of the magazine's creators and writers, an undercur-rent that favored whiteness informed narratives of and around fashion in the publication. As might be expected, the rhythm unit-ing these three dance partners (white bodies, the African Ameri-can cultural elite, and the African American working class) would resonate with an uneven, discordant beat.

For example, according to an article written for the magazine by African American clubwoman and political activist Mary Church Terrell: "Every woman, no matter what her circumstances, owes it to herself, her family and her friends to look as well as her means will permit."[5] In a striking example of the ways in which elite African American women would attempt to define the impor-tance of fashion for other groups of African American women, Terrell makes clear that more than individual preference is at stake in how an African American women dresses. How such women appear in public bears not just upon her, but upon her family, her friends, and indeed, the entire African American race. In a further effort to make clear that economic means bear no relationship to one's ability to understand and embrace a fitting fashion statement, the article goes on to suggest that "[h]ats that are modest and becoming are just as cheap as those which attract disagreeable attention" and ends with an admonition to women to always be mindful of appearing less than demure "because of the excruciating discord between the color of the trimmings and the complexion of the wearers."[6] Terrell's article draws together the pieces of an argument about the relationship of race, class, and morality to fashion in the magazine. She makes clear that African Americans in a higher social category have the right and responsibility to share their views with those in less secure cir-cumstances.

In the next issue of the magazine, at least one reader applauded Terrell's sentiments. The letter writer, Mrs. Sarah Mitchell of Cleveland, Ohio, points out that such thinking is necessary and right, given the "inability of the lower social classes to take advantage of opportunities presented at their very door." She goes on to bemoan the fact that any work aimed at helping the lower classes often becomes "a disagreeable enterprise" and ends with the suggestion that they should probably have to "allow a generation or two to pass before we expect to see any results from our labor."[7] Disagreeable or not, those involved with *Ringwood's Journal* continued to advocate the uplifting of the lower classes of African Americans, though much of what they would suggest involved little more than allowing such groups to spend time in their company.

Accordingly, in an article that further explores the relationship of the social elite to the rest of the African American female population, an unnamed writer suggests that the problems of all African Americans would be solved if more young women would turn to their betters as examples and for advice. In presenting a case for more women joining her organization, she writes that once it gets off the ground, the members' chief aim "would be to gather under their wing as many young women as possible, whose minds should be enlightened, whose fingers trained and whose sentiments elevated by personal contact with cultured, refined women." If she is successful, she believes "the race problem would be on the high road to solution."[8] The articles written by African American women, as well as the fashion pages featuring Whites, would tell nonelite African American women that their fashion choices reverberated with the possibility of attaining cultural respectability and respect. This language—of fashion's ability to make an African American woman into a lady whose appearance was capable of refuting cultural charges of immorality—dominated the magazine.

SHOWING AND PROVING THAT THEY WERE LADIES

In the gentle rustle of a skirt swishing around a neatly hidden ankle lay a possible answer to cultural charges and beliefs about African

American women's sexual proclivities. The painful clutch of a tightly laced corset announced a long-sought-after modesty. A hat chosen to blend with an ensemble, evidence of fashionable taste, denoted a belated acceptance into a members-only cult of "true womanhood." At the end of the nineteenth century, although fashion was discussed as a marker of class status for all women, this was particularly true for African Americans. Its function, according to the editor and writers in *Ringwood's Journal,* was part of a larger project aimed at refuting charges of African American moral inferiority and distancing African American women from cultural associations with rape and sexual availability.

While much of the publication argues that the legacies of enslavement continue to haunt African Americans of both genders, by far the majority of advice is directed at African American women and urges them to adhere to increased standards of morality and virtue. These were areas in which their readers had been damaged by enslavement, according to the magazine. As one article argues: "Women who eschew the garish and gaudy in dress may demand more consideration and respect that those who violate this principle. The fact must be especially impressed upon our young women of the South who are constantly exposed to the depravity and lechery of the fair-skinned destroyers whose hearts are blacker than Erebus." The article goes on to list the styles and colors that indicate sexual unavailability and moral steadfastness (red is particularly forbidden, as is anything fringed), complete with illustrations and dress patterns. It ends with the charge to any young women who might be reading to "array themselves modestly and tastefully and urge their companions to do the same" (2). This sentiment is echoed in another article entitled "Plain Talks to Our Girls," from the same May/June 1893 issue, which admonishes young African American women for an inappropriate and immodest sense of fashion that leads them to experience what the writer describes as "disagreeable attention" (17).

The single-minded focus by many elite African Americans on attempting to fit themselves into nineteenth-century constructions and ideologies of ladyhood was motivated in large part by a desire to replace dominant cultural assertions of the group as primarily understood through their bodily associations with sex and rape with narratives that proved them to be middle class and, as a result, pious, chaste, modern, and worthy of attaining the supposed advantages of membership in the cult of domesticity. Such an analysis connected where African American women lived, the clubs to which they belonged, the people for whom they worked, and how they dressed to an effort aimed at controlling public perceptions of their uncertain virtue. Toward that end, one of the magazine's favored strategies for introducing short biographies was to list the educational achievement, bearing, beauty, and moral hallmarks of the subject. These topics were generally accompanied by an explicit reference to the woman under discussion as deserving of the title "lady." In one such biography, from the May/June issue of 1893, Julia Mason is described as "divinely tall, with a pleasant countenance, illuminated by a pair of bright, purposeful eyes." In addition to her numerous affiliations with various organizations like the Baptist Convention, the Colored Woman's League, and the advisory board of the Bethel Literary and Historical Society, we are told that in June 1890, Mason "was a delegate to the International Sabbath School convention . . . with the distinction of being the only visiting colored lady delegate among the sixteen hundred" (4). While referring to such a woman as a lady might seem unimportant, it becomes more significant once we recognize that this one instance is the only time in the publication that the appellation "lady" is used to describe an African American woman.

That one instance, along with the biography's careful attention to Mason's appearance and bearing, signals readers that this woman is much more than a simple news figure. Indeed, she is part of a larger project of identifying for others, as well as themselves, which African American women should be considered ladies, what that term means to African American women in general, and how fashion could play a role in its designation. This last was accomplished in no small part by the inclusion of an

5. Susie I. Lankford Shorter,
a "lady"

image that showed the clothing, jewelry, and hairstyle that helped
make an African American woman a lady.

While biographies that described the look and social affiliations of the subject were one means for explaining why they were
to be accorded special significance, other areas of accomplishment
were also worthy of notice. In the first few sentences of a lengthy
obituary of Mrs. Reverend Joseph Thompson, we are told: "She
was an exceptional woman in many respects; amiable, pious,
devout. She was a great organizer and had wonderful executive
ability." The obituary goes on to say she helped those who had
been enslaved during the antebellum period escape and that
"[d]uring the dark days of slavery her mind was riveted on the
work of allaying the suffering of her unfortunate fellow associates. Many clever schemes she devised in effecting their escape"
(6). Not only did Mrs. Thompson possess the qualities of an
undisputed member of the "cult of true womanhood" (piety, ami-
ability, and religious devotion), but also she married a reverend
and had helped rescue those who had been enslaved. It is then
surprising that she is referred to as a "woman" as opposed to a
"lady." In any case, as with Julia Mason, an image once again
draws attention to the fashion choices, as well as grooming

6. Mrs. Thompson obituary
portrait

details, of someone whom the magazine has chosen to feature. In the extant issues of the magazine, Mrs. Thompson would stand as the lone image of an African American woman who did not have light skin and white features.

While it should be clear that for *Ringwood's Journal*, "lady-hood" often went hand-in-hand with a politics of color and exceptionalism, the publication needed to craft a narrative of inclusion, given that the magazine was aimed at a wider reading public. Accordingly, the project of defining and identifying "lady-hood" included and was indeed exemplified by its advertisements. Here, there is a consistent narrative about the possibility of and for African American respectability that goes beyond the designation "woman." A close reading of the advertisements reveals a model of and for African American femininity and narratives of thrift, hard work, and respectability as a backdrop to the more pointed discussion about fashion. In addition, the advertisements stroke the readers' egos by addressing them as "queens," "ladies," and "of culture." Whether or not one believed these sentiments, the magazine made a point of addressing its readership as if it were refined, or interested in refinement.

ADVERTISING LADYHOOD

The one or two pages of (business-card-size) advertising in each of the two extant issues of the magazine provide quite a bit of information about its imagined readership. Most ads are for boardinghouses that specialize in "first-class services" for African Americans looking for places to live in urban areas. They range from simple declarations ("Mrs. Daniel Hynson, Boarding and Lodging" in Providence, R.I.) to more elaborate presentations from women who ran such establishments in New York and Boston.

These last make sure to mention the quality of service, and Mrs. Mary L. Jackson in Boston notes that her establishment is "first class" and offers an "intelligence office" (postal services) and board (meals) for customers, whether or not they choose to room with her. Others, like the ad from Mrs. D. Whitehurst for the Clarendon House on West Twenty-seventh Street in New York City (then the heart of the African American community), announce that they are "patronized by the public from all sections of the country" (79). We can assume that these establishments were meeting the housing needs of African American men and women who wanted clean and safe places to stay as they migrated out of the South and into the urban areas of the Northeast. Indeed, although the magazine itself was published in the Midwest, all the boardinghouses advertised in its pages are in the North. At the very least, we know that the African American women who owned and ran the boardinghouses believed themselves to be refined, hardworking, and respectable. They are almost living, breathing examples of the political ideologies expressed in the magazine. Given that the advertisements for their businesses are surrounded by ads that discuss fashion, the relationship of the magazine to an emerging discourse on fashion is not difficult to fathom. It was firmly connected to a larger political project that involved foregrounding the morality of African American women much more generally.

Apart from advertisements for "respectable" boarding establishments run by African American women, advertisements for fashion magazines and pamphlets predominate. It wasn't until after 1893 that magazines secured most of their revenue from advertisements rather than from subscriptions, and most offer some incentive to subscribers. In addition, most offer readers the opportunity to make money by selling subscriptions to the magazine's readership. The advertisement asking readers to subscribe to a pamphlet published by *Ringwood's Journal* entitled "The Queen of Fashion" is the second largest on the page. It tells readers that this pamphlet, collected from information from past issues of *Ringwood's Journal*, is needed for its practical hints. It goes on to add, "Women of Culture Particularly Commend It" and shouts in large bold letters, "This Is an Invitation to You, Lady, to You." The adjacent advertisement for *Ringwood's Journal* notes that "The Queen of Fashion" is specifically for "medium sized fashion figures" and will be sent to any dressmaker for one year for the price of one dollar if only they will subscribe to the journal.

These types of advertisements are rounded out by one asking readers to subscribe to the *New York Age,* "An Afro-American Journal of News and Opinion. Four to Eight Pages, Devoted to Race Interests, General News, and Literature," and another asking for subscriptions to a volume entitled *Women of Distinction* published by L. A. Scruggs that explores the lives of African American women said to be "Remarkable in Works and Invincible in Character." A number of the women involved with beginning the magazine have entries in the volume. As a result, the advertisements link fashion with character, morality, and acceptable gender practices. They also ask us to think more deeply about the role and place of whiteness in the context of African American women's turn-of-the-century fashion practices.

Accordingly, the last two advertisements on the page are from white companies associated with the journal. One is for the monthly *Chaperone Magazine,* which was published from the Chaperone Building in St. Louis, Missouri, between 1888 and 1898 by Annie L. Orff. It was devoted to a bit of everything, listing arts, music, literature, science, home organization, dress, the

7. Advertisements, *Ringwood's Journal*, 1893

children, cuisine, and humor on its cover. The advertisement shouts that readers may receive both *Ringwood's Journal* and *Chaperone Magazine* for only two dollars per year. The last advertisement on the page is also from a white company who did quite a bit of business with *Ringwood's Journal*. The Jenness Miller Company, based in New York, provided many of the illustrations and dressmaking patterns found in the magazine. Here they advertise subscriptions to the *Jenness Miller Illustrated Monthly* as well as a copy of the company's *Comprehensive Physical Culture*, written by Mabel Jenness.

This last is particularly interesting, as Jenness Miller was a proponent of dress reform and quite active in the social movement aimed at abolishing the corset, as well as other types of constraining and confining "fashionable" dress that purportedly led to poor health and posture and interfered with the mental well-being of all middle-class American women.[9] A worldwide movement with proponents in France, Germany, and Great Britain that began in the 1850s, its U.S. manifestation was the only one with a large following among the middle class and, it appears in at least this one instance, among African American women. Given that the thinking at the time and in recent scholarship generally sug-

8. Jenness-Miller artistic clothing line, *Ringwood's Journal*, 1893

gests that African American women were neither addressed by the movement nor thought to have had any interest in it, it is significant to find that *Ringwood's Journal* was very much involved in addressing the issue. At the same time, however, the magazine included dress patterns and articles of the sort the dress reform movement opposed. *Ringwood's Journal* offered African American women choices, options, and exposure to differing ideas and debates about the meaning and use of fashion in relation to status and American culture.

Fashion, *Ringwood's Journal* readers are told, offers an opportunity to engage in political activity; fashion offers the ability to "uplift" African Americans in a lower socioeconomic group; fashion can erase the stain of an unsavory past. It is, however, key, that with the exception of the obituary for Mrs. Thompson already mentioned, the only representations of women described as fashionably attired "ladies" are either understood to be, or appear to be, white.

WHITE FASHION, BLACK READERS

Given that the images used to portray the magazine's formal discussion of fashion and fashionable clothes were of white women, let me turn to the meanings of race, status, and fashion history in relation to white bodies, contextualized by the blackness of the magazine's owners, editors, and readers.

EQUESTRIENNE TIGHTS.

"The Russian Cossack" (reprinted from *Frank Leslie's Weekly*) describes the visit to New York by a group of "representatives of the world's ruling race." They were so described due to their origins in the Caucasus Mountains and, as a result, "having beauty and courage as inalienable rights of birth." We are also told that for them was named the white race that "predominates the world over." The Cossacks, however, had fallen on hard times. Twenty years before their visit to New York, they had been conquered and enslaved by the czar of Russia. They had come to the United States on tour to raise money and had proved, if the article is correct, to be quite a hit. The article turns toward a discussion of how, though enslaved, this once proud and historically significant group had to learn to function as a "race without a country." They managed to overcome their disadvantaged circumstance because they were "great swordsmen" and had as a result "become of service to the Russian Czar and were of much use in battle" (17).

After fully detailing the attire (extremely colorful, homespun, and practical) of the visiting delegation of twelve, the article goes on to tell readers: "They are passionately fond of ornaments, and only live to fight, drink wine and adorn themselves" (17). Indeed, as the translator explains it, they are visiting New York because as a group, the Cossacks "have very little money in their country. They have no money at all of their own and come into possession of very little Russian money. . . . All the gold and silver they get is immediately converted into ornaments" (19). In short, the article details the visit of a poor, landless group of slaves who disdain to work, love to drink wine, are violent, and are most concerned with self-adornment—a depiction strikingly similar to that found

9. A fashion page, *Ringwood's Journal*

enness=Miller Artistic Clothing.

THE MATERNITY   NO. 277—THE MATERNITY   THE MATERNITY DIVIDED   THE EQUESTRIENNI
EMILETTE.   GOWN FORM.   SKIRT.   TIGHTS.

in the magazine's discussions of the behavioral legacies of enslavement for African Americans. Though written for a mainstream
magazine, the article provides an ironic counterpoint to racial
narratives that ascribe these very same behaviors to African
Americans due solely to their African heritage and enslaved past.
The article is followed by a fashion page that portrays white
women as models of the latest fashionable styles.

Fashion in *Ringwood's Journal* was not easily separated from
discussions of and beliefs about modesty, chastity, and character.[10]
Those under discussion could be white peasants, new migrants
from the southern United States, or politically and socially conscious members of women's clubs. What they all had in common
was how they drew connections between what they wore and the
values and statements their apparel choices made about their
entire race, class, and gender. Fashion in the nineteenth century
would also presume a white standard bearer of and for a fashionable message. That whiteness could be worn on an African American body with light skin and white features (like the editors and
writers for the magazine), or on a body that was understood to be
white (like those pictured in the lithographs about dress reform).
In either instance, whiteness predominated.

If fashion was discussed in this magazine as a mirror or indicator of internal standards of morality, it was just as surely viewed
as an external manifestation of class standing. This dichotomy
was clearly important to turn-of-the-century public figures like
Alice Dunbar-Nelson, who once wrote in her diary that Philadel-
phian Addie Dickerson, a clubwoman and head of the Republican
Council of Colored Women at the time, "looked tattered, un-
mended, and ungroomed."[11] Not only did Dickinson's unkempt
state speak to her personal condition, but also her class status and
membership in the elite group of African American women like
those involved with *Ringwood's Journal* should have precluded
her appearing in public in such a state.[12] Dunbar-Nelson was not
alone in her attention to the presentation of fashion for African
American women. The magazine offered a means of satisfying
both readers considered "ladies" and those less sure about the

designation's applying to them. Vexingly, however, while the magazine included numerous images of African American women who were members of the cultural and political elite as models of acceptable, even exalted, examples of African American "ladyhood," it primarily offered images of white bodies as acceptable examples of fashion proper. A discussion about and representation of race and fashion that privileged African American women would have to wait for another century and, indeed, another magazine altogether. That publication was *Half-Century Magazine*.

FASHIONING RACE: THE TWENTIETH CENTURY

Fashion had long held particular implications for African American women. In the nineteenth century, *Ringwood's Journal* inaugurated a gendered discussion and representation of fashion for African American female readers; *Half-Century Magazine* broadened and repositioned the concerns expressed by its predecessor. Fashion and style would no longer function to erase memories of African American women's rape during the antebellum period. By the first few decades of the twentieth century, speaking about fashion would cease to be a complicated conversation about the race or skin color of the body most ably qualified to represent it. Instead, given the realities of urbanization and migration, fashion would come to represent an opportunity to control the behavior of African Americans.

At first glance, it may not be easy to discern the connection between *Ringwood's Journal*, a turn-of-the-century African American woman's magazine whose underlying narrative turned upon the presence and meaning of rape in the lives of formerly enslaved biracial African American women, and a later publication that sought to more firmly position African American women in an early-twentieth-century rhetoric of urbanization, modernity, and domesticity. The images evoked by these two constructions of African American womanhood as either sexually available rape victim or chaste morally upstanding homemaker are at opposite ends of a spectrum, with little to buffer in between. Yet at the turn

of the century, these two images were at the very least intercon-
nected, if not completely dependent on one another.

Moving from the unfortunate victim of white sexual aggression
and power to the stylishly attired homemaker, fashion would
come to denote, at the turn of the century, different worlds of
meaning and understanding. But the meanings of fashion and its
relationship to respectability would bind the two periods for
decades to come. These two magazines chart a shift in the rhetoric and focus of popular magazines aimed at African American
women in urban areas at the turn of the century. While during the
late nineteenth century, *Ringwood's Journal* was dominated by
African American women's club movement luminaries, as well as
by women who came of age in an environment that necessitated
their working through issues of rape in their lives and the lives of
their mothers, *Half-Century Magazine* sought to weave its story
from a different, more "modern" fiber that emphasized the cultural project of uplift in relation to fashion, race, and adornment
in the context of African American migration out of the South.

By the second decade of the twentieth century, fashion was no
longer discussed as a means to erase the cultural memory of an
unfortunate past; rather it would become a symbol of the inten-
tion to fully define and explore a new, more modern future. The
twentieth century would suggest that fashion, adornment, and
public display were most significant as markers of a northern,
urban, modern understanding of who African American women
were. Here the bogeyman, as opposed to fashion choices that
reinforced cultural associations about African American women
and sex, is most consistently the uncivilized character of newly
arrived southern migrants who occupy the buses, street corners,
and other public spaces of urban America.

4

"Colored Faces Looking Out of Fashion Plates. Well!"

Twentieth-Century Fashion, Migration, and Urbanization

The woman who worships at the shrine of fashion loses her bearings among the perplexities of our modern life. She has no time to read good books, no time to cultivate those things that minister to the refinement and beauty of her home, and no time or inclination to contribute her heart and talents to the social uplift of those around her.

—*Fannie Barrier Williams, 1913*

IN the pages of the nineteenth-century *Ringwood's Journal*, fashion for African American women was most often discussed as a means of uplifting the African American race as a whole and distancing African American women from outmoded associations with slavery, violence, and sexual vulnerability. Fashion's relevance was consistently invoked by those desirous of donning the mantle of "ladyhood," and fashionable display was described as a crucial prerequisite for inhabiting public spaces such as churches, political meetings, and social events. Disturbingly, the models of "fashionability" most often portrayed in the magazine had light skin and white features. In the nineteenth century, fashion was most consistently connected with those who were members of the African American elite; business owners, clubwomen, and holders of titles as the first African American to reach a particular goal made up the bulk of those pictured in that magazine.

With the widespread African American migration to the urban North and Midwest in the early decades of the twentieth century, both the discussion and display of fashion moved from pages of publications like *Ringwood's Journal* and the attendant realms of the African American elite to the less elite "public spaces" of front stoops, neighborhood street corners, and trolley cars in urban Philadelphia, Chicago, and New York. The streets around commercial areas in African American communities came to be described as "strolls," and evening and weekend walks to show off new clothes were a popular activity for migrating working-class African American men and women.[1] As Virginia Wolcott has pointed out: "Because public displays were crucial to the enactment of respectability, the city was often the theater in which the drama of respectability was most elaborately performed. . . . In urban neighborhoods, potent symbols such as clothing, mode of transportation, or the state of a front yard or stoop signaled the level of respectability to others."[2] These public displays hardly sat well with elite groups of African American women. While fashion became a key element in the process of assimilating into existing African American communities, as well as of reinventing personal, more modern urban identities, it also became central in the battle to define and control the public image of certain African Americans.

Half-Century Magazine communicated meanings about and understandings of fashion and style to a twentieth-century reading audience. At the same time, it tells a story about how the passage of time and the movement of people into urban areas came to broaden the visual representation of fashionable African American women to include those who were not white, elite, or exceptional. The new century would herald a fashion defined by the struggle between those who believed it was tied to notions of status and respectability and, as a result, of primary importance

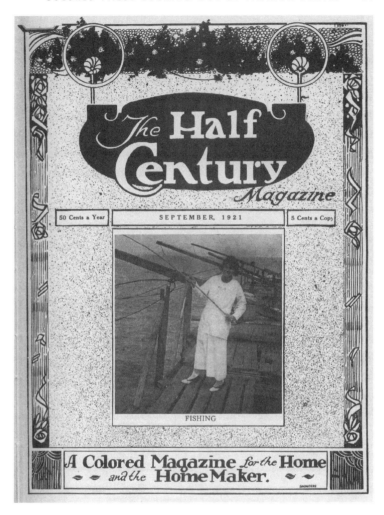

10. *Half-Century* cover, September 1921

when displayed in public spaces, and others who thought it had little to do with status or respectability and everything to do with the democratically seductive and liberating nature of a new, modern urban milieu. For both groups, fashion would be key. The conflict was over the nature of the lock most in need of opening.

At the beginning of the twentieth century, fashion, urbanization, respectability, and public space were inextricably linked in the minds of many. This was certainly the case in *Half-Century Magazine*, where the changes in controlling ideas about the significance of fashion that were a result of African American migration, and that movement along with urbanization, took center stage. This magazine, with its African American female readership, writers, and editorial board, was one of the leading indicators of the changes on the horizon. Though many scholars have noted the role the African American press (most notably the *Chicago Defender*) played in encouraging African American migration, few if any have examined the role of that press in helping migrants adjust to northern society. This was one of the implicit functions of *Half-Century Magazine*, and fashion and its meaning would play a central role in that adjustment.

Half-Century Magazine

Given that it benefited from a general rise in rates of literacy for African Americans and from the increasing pace of African American migration to the urban North, *Half-Century Magazine* entered the marketplace under far more favorable conditions than had *Ringwood's Journal* in the previous century. In addition to having women as the editors and publisher, compared to many other African American periodicals of the age, *Half-Century Magazine's* nine years in existence (1916–1925) surpass those of the majority of previous African American magazines and place it among the likes of *The Colored American Magazine* (1900–1909), *Crisis* (1910–1940), *The Messenger* (1917–1928), and *Opportunity* (1923–1939) in terms of longevity. That *Half-Century Magazine* has virtually been ignored is somewhat surprising.

Its owner and editor in chief from 1916 to 1925 was Katherine Williams.[3] Born on December 31, 1894, in Nehawka, Nebraska, Williams moved to Chicago with her parents while still a teenager.[4] She was twenty-two years old when she assumed the reins of *Half-Century Magazine* and wrote her first editorial, which introduced the new publication to her audience in August 1916. In it, Williams went to some lengths to make clear that the

11. *Half-Century* editor Katherine Williams, 1917

magazine would aim at a niche different from that occupied by other publications. Most specifically, she wanted the new magazine to be for a popular audience made up primarily of "the masses." In a not-so-veiled reference to the National Association for the Advancement of Colored People's *Crisis,* edited by W.E.B. Du Bois, Williams tells readers her magazine should be given a chance in part because it "is not an organ of any cause, religion, sect, or propaganda." To ensure that her point is not missed, she goes on to add, "Our policy calls for specialization, not 'Along the Color Line,' but along other and equally essential lines." That those "equally essential" lines would include discussions of class is quickly made clear when Williams goes on to further distinguish the intended readership for the publication by making sure readers understand: "It will not be our ambition to make this magazine a 'literary gem' either for our own gratification or to suit the fancy of the 'high-brows,' but to present facts in plain, commonsense language, so that the masses may read and understand; or in the words of Brother Taylor, we propose to call a 'spade a *spade*' and not an 'excavating instrument for manual manipulation'" (1).

Published in Chicago, *Half-Century Magazine* took its name from the fifty years since the Emancipation Proclamation had freed African Americans from enslavement. While reliable circulation figures are impossible to obtain, some scholars have estimated that they reached as high as sixteen thousand copies per month (though the magazine itself put this number closer to forty-two thousand).⁵ In addition, the number of actual readers is difficult to pinpoint accurately, given the oft-bemoaned practice on the part of many of the magazine's readers of sharing copies with each other, reading them in beauty shops, neighbors' homes, and standing at newsstands. Despite the fact that the editorial group chose to send out free sample issues of *Half-Century Magazine* during the first few months of the magazine's publication, by February 1917, Williams unleashed a scathing rebuke aimed at those she believed to be reading the magazine without paying for it. In an attempt to discourage such practices, she wrote a scolding editorial entitled "Live and Let Live." She begins by informing readers, "If your neighbor is getting the *Half-Century* regularly each month—your neighbor is paying for it" (3).

After explaining to any to whom it may be unclear that one gets nothing in life for free, Williams goes on to list many of the underappreciated costs associated with producing the publication: "It *costs* to print the magazine on the very highest grade of paper that can be secured. It *costs* to get the brown-skin color scheme on the Cover. It *costs* to make the Fashion Page attractive for 'mi-lady'—oh, how it costs! It *costs* to settle the Printer's monthly bill—whew, it costs like—Well, it *costs and costs*! . . . If the magazine is worth reading, it is also worth paying for. . . . *So why not pay for it? Why not live and let live?*" (emphasis in original; ibid.). It would appear that Williams's words struck a chord, as the publication flourished for another eight years.

From 1916 to 1918 the magazine was subtitled the "Colored Monthly for the Business Man and the Home Maker," and the editorial content was evenly divided between business and home-making, but after a few years it reduced its size and cost, dropped much of the emphasis on business, and labeled itself "A Colored Magazine for the Home and Home Maker." This name change signaled a shift to a focus on women, and an editorial strategy aimed almost entirely at that group. Given the repeated calls for support from subscribers, it is not difficult to imagine that the change in size and cost was necessitated by a desire to make the magazine more profitable. It is significant that the owner and publisher of the magazine soon ascertained that a focus on women would accomplish her aims.[6]

Early issues contained about twenty pages, with roughly one-third of the publication taken up by advertisements. The remainder was comprised of short fiction, biographical sketches, serialized novels, editorials, and a number of columns that discussed etiquette, domestic science, life in Chicago, and, of course, fashion. In listing the eight reasons why African American women should subscribe to the magazine, the publication tells readers that it is necessary for those who wish: "1. To conduct your home more easily and more cheaply. 2. To dress smartly at the lowest cost. 3. To read the best stories by the leading Colored writers. 4. To bring up and train your children better. 5. To see our own beautiful women depicted in the latest and smartest costumes of Dame Fashion. 6. To know the most novel ideas for entertaining. 7. To be a leader in the social life of your community. 8. To keep in touch with all that is newest and most vital in women's interests, inside and outside the home" (December 1917, 8)

The list can be considered an outline of the beliefs held by the magazine's editor about the advice most needed by certain groups and classes of African Americans more than a guide to readers. The magazine wanted its readership to be interested in saving money, dressing well, running a home efficiently. The editorial content of the magazine makes clear that Williams believed far too many readers were unclear about the importance of these activities. Accordingly, she consistently offered similar advice to newly arrived migrants to urban areas, whom she believed ill-equipped to handle the demands of living in such a new and different environment. Further, given that she chose to aim her content at the so-called African American "masses," we might assume that they are the group to whom she is most consistently speaking.

For example, an editorial also written by Williams in the August–September 1920 issue titled "Are We Our Brothers' Keepers" complains, "Many members of the race lack respect for conventionalities, decorum, and even common decency in public places." As one of many examples of this lack, she goes on to say. "When the weather is hot, half naked men and women, some minus their shoes and stockings, sit around in the windows, on the porches and steps, or lounge on the curbstone in front of the house." As an antidote for such behavior, the writer concludes: "Our women should be taught to wear becoming clothes, they cost no more than the other kind. Both men and women could be taught the importance of keeping neat and clean—especially should they be urged to keep tidy on the street. . . . The race as a whole could be taught to be quiet and polite in public places" (3).

At the core of the advice about fashion in the magazine is a struggle to understand and control the changes wrought by the wholesale migration of African Americans to urban areas, as well as a desire to instruct the migrants about what the elite of their race expect from them when they arrive. As Dwight Brooks has noted, most African American editors and writers in northern periodicals saw a good part of their task as setting and defining the terms of citizenship for this new group of migrants.[7] If true, for African American women, fashion was one of the key dictates to which they were urged to attend. Many African Americans who had been living in urban areas since before the Great Migration identified themselves as middle class and constructed representations of themselves that portrayed them as educated, refined, and forward thinking. New migrants, however, were often discussed and spoken to as if they were lower class and therefore uncivilized, or lacking in the basic skills they would need to be considered upstanding members of "the race." *Half-Century Magazine* set out to provide all who read it with what it believed to be much-needed help in negotiating a new environment. To be sure, the embodiment of respectability was also central to the definition of the middle class in the dominant culture. Numerous scholars have noted the increase in the number of etiquette manuals and other prescriptive works aimed at controlling the behavior of women and at defining acceptable clothing styles and etiquette on urban streets and in private parlors.[8] These displays of respectability were firmly tied to notions of domesticity that precluded white women from working outside the home. However, African American women were often chastised for displays in public places that were tied to their having to work.

Hazel Carby has argued that the migration of working-class African American women from rural to urban areas fomented a number of "moral panics" on the part of the middle class. Focusing on how various discourses positioned the sexual behavior of migrant working women as a threat to the establishment of stable communities in the North, she argues that these women were viewed as a danger to social order. This focus on "proper behavior," clothing, and deportment, then, became a prerequisite for middle-class status in African American communities.[9]

Given the numbers of readers from various regions of the country that wrote to the editor of *Half-Century Magazine* to sing its praises, it would certainly seem that the time was right for a publication that would focus so specifically on such subject matter. While some of these letters went on at length, chronicling their reaction to every story, column, and article, others were quite short and to the point. Mrs. William Henderson of Springfield, Ohio, reported that she loved the entire issue of the magazine she had read and stated simply, "Send me some more" (October 1916, 18). Although Mrs. Henderson does not go so far as to tell us what about the magazine in particular caught her interest, it is not difficult to believe that given the consistency with which the relationship between urbanity and fashion was featured, this was likely somewhere in the equation.

THE MIGRATION OF FASHION

In letter after letter, one article after the other, editorial after editorial, *Half-Century Magazine* is full of anecdotal evidence of the fashion concerns the African American elite held about those who had recently migrated or were members of the working class. For example, in an article from the September–October issue of 1922, entitled "Judging by Your Clothes What Do People Think of You?" the author, known simply as "The Investigator," suggests that as she walks through the streets of Chicago she cannot help but be shocked by the number of young women who "show a crying need of help in the selection of a costume." She goes on: "I passed a young woman one morning not long ago, who wore a pink gingham dress, the cut of which told me [it] was intended for wear in the kitchen only. . . . Her brown shoes were of the Egyptian sandal variety, very much in need of polish and run down at the heels. . . . Another woman passed me a few minutes later who made me wonder if hers was a house without mirrors" (19).[10]

Far from an isolated lament, this would appear to echo the experience of others living in Chicago who had to look at those who did not share certain sensibilities, a bit of a fashion nightmare for many of the contributors to the magazine. They deemed women they encountered out and about in the city to be dressed as if they had no idea of what was appropriate, or as if attempting to imitate the less desirable elements found in cities. Mariah Johnson of Chicago wrote to the "People's Forum" section of the magazine to report that she works nights and often sees "pretty young Colored girls on the streets and in taxicabs just going home. These girls are imitating nearly as possible in dress and manners the women of the underworld and those notorious women whose pictures appear on the front page of newspapers daily" (July–August 1923, 21).

As a result of shifts in the numbers of human bodies occupying urban spaces, by the early twentieth century, fashion's meaning would simultaneously expand and contract. On the one hand, those who were portrayed as and discussed as a part of fashionable discourse would expand to include a range of African American womanhood. Not just the elite members of "the race" or those with light skin and white features would be portrayed and imaged as employing a fashionable corporeal message. Rather, large-boned, dark-skinned women would be represented as the primary purveyors of fashion's message. On the other hand, the meaning of fashion would come to be narrowly construed as most important in relation to African American women in public spaces, bounded by urban areas. As was true with other areas of advice offered in the magazine, the working classes, as well as new migrants from the South, would be offered increasingly urgent advice about fashion and its uses and frequent misuses in their new home.

For example, in an effort to acknowledge the difficulty, for African American women who lived some distance from large cities, of shopping for and obtaining many of the more appropriate clothes, fashions, and styles featured in the magazine, by October 1916 (two months after its start), *Half-Century Magazine* began a shopping department whose sole function was to purchase non-perishable products not available to rural and southern African American women. The announcement about the service begins with a large banner headline asking, "May we shop for you?" adding that this is the "Practical Side of *Half-Century Magazine*."

> If you do not live in a large city with a great variety of shops, you cannot always buy whatever you want. *The Half-Century Magazine* with its offices in the center of Chicago's shopping district and with Miss Jane Hudson on its staff can always help you. Whenever you want anything not instantly found in your local stores, simply send check or money order, payable to *Half-Century Magazine* to cover the cost of the article ordered to Miss Hudson, and she will do your purchasing without charge for her service. (15)

Circulation figures jumped dramatically a few months after the service began.

The success of the shopping service may have been a response to the desire of readers to emulate the fashionable attire of the African American women pictured on the cover of the magazine, as well as in its fashion pages. But it is just as possible that those who shaped the magazine's content wanted to ensure that women migrating to the city would have appropriate clothes when they arrived and save the writers of the magazine the horror of looking at them otherwise attired. The success of the shopping service could also easily have been due to its use by African American women who lived in urban areas and wanted to avoid the indignity associated with shopping for clothes in white department stores, where African American women were often denied access to dressing rooms and were frequently the last to be waited on if there were white customers in the stores at the same time. Indeed, given that procuring many of the fashions touted in the magazine would have involved either shopping in stores owned by whites but located in African American communities, or leaving African American communities to purchase the featured outfits, the inauguration of a shopping service was more than likely welcomed by women in urban areas, as well as by those planning to migrate to them.

In addition to promoting its shopping service, the magazine was not above including "hand-holding" hints to lead readers to its desired conclusion about the primacy of fashion. In March 1920, the opening page of the magazine includes a written conversation between a fictional Mrs. Smith and her good friend. The two women marvel at how consistently a third neighbor, the equally fictitious Lydia James, is able to appear in the latest styles. She is said to wear dresses months and seasons before they make it to the department stores. One friend tells the other that this is because she is a regular reader of *Half-Century Magazine* and, as a result, is always sure just what outfits will make the best statements. Mrs. Smith goes on: "Mrs. James has been taking it for years, but she didn't tell anyone because she is so selfish that she wanted to keep the good news all to herself. See, here is the fashion page; these are the advance styles—summer styles and it is only January" (3).

One's fashion sensibility, the magazine suggested, was the subject of conversation, and if one wanted to be held in high regard, like Lydia James, they had best subscribe to, or at least buy a copy of, *Half-Century Magazine*. Not doing so meant risking all manner of spying and gossip by strangers who would then write up their observations in a popular magazine, as well as neighbors who would discuss their observations closer to home. Whatever the motivation, the magazine's editorial content clearly went to some lengths to emphasize the urgency of adhering to certain notions of fashionable attire. Its concern with fashion is exceeded only by the visual representation of fashion on the publication's covers. Interestingly, *Half-Century Magazine*'s resolve to represent suitably attired African American women on the cover would multiply the types of women who could model how fashion could and should look. While this consistent focus on fashion tells us quite a bit about its ubiquitous nature at the turn of the century, it also exemplifies a fixation that drew strong criticism from more than a few quarters.

At the end of the nineteenth century, *Ringwood's Journal* proclaimed that fashion's dictates were a necessary prerequisite for the daunting task of culturally and socially uplifting African Americans beyond the historical grip of slavery. By the first few decades of the twentieth century, African American women began to hear that they had learned this lesson a bit too well. It was now time, at least one commentor would opine, to cease worshipping "at the shrine of fashion," as the practice of that particular religion had begun to take time, attention, and interest away from the very notion of uplift to which it had so recently been connected. For example, in the epigraph that begins this chapter, Fannie Barrier Williams urges African American women of all social levels to turn their collective backs on what she believed to be the "low-brow" pursuit of fashion and to rededicate themselves to the higher callings of education and homemaking. In 1913 Williams described this phenomenon as "the dress burden" and concluded that it had come about as the result of living in an "age of extravagance and greed for luxuries." She tells readers that she was moved to write because the "passion for ornamentation and display debilitates our moral as well as our physical strength."[11]

In contrast to nineteenth-century concerns with instructing nonelite African American women about the role of fashion in their lives, Williams points out: "It cannot be said that only women of weak and frivolous minds are 'crazy about dress,' for church women, women interested in public questions and trained for social service are all more or less inoculated with the virus of 'style' and dress display." Fashion, she believed, had become a significant impediment to change and social growth, as those seduced by its allure spent significant amounts of time and money focused on its procurement. The single-minded pursuit of fashion was, she suggested, indicative of the pitfalls inherent in the more modern cultural surroundings of African Americans.[12] If the cover of *Half-Century Magazine* and indeed the magazine as a whole are any indication, her calls for change were largely unheeded.

THE BURDEN OF DRESS

In the opening years of the twenty-first century, we know with a certainty born of familiarity that images of African Americans may on any given day, afternoon, or evening appear before our collective gaze on the cover and in the pages of a magazine. Whether they are models, sports figures, or celebrities, the occurrence rarely causes more than a ripple in our cultural consciousness. In the early twentieth century however, such occurrences were much more infrequent. Indeed, one of the striking features of *Half-Century Magazine* is its often-remarked-upon use of African American women on its cover.[13] The cover of a magazine is no small thing. It is the magazine's most important advertisement, the packaging that helps readers decide to purchase it over another publication.

One of the key changes heralded by the advent of *Half-Century Magazine* was its liberal use of African American models on all its covers and in the pages of its fashion section. It also illustrated much of the serialized fiction with scenes that featured African

American women. Yet fashion still posed vexing questions. Here, the tilt of a hat, length of a skirt, or height of a shoe heel were disconnected from concerns over modesty, piety, and morality and instead spoke volumes about regional, urban, and classed displays of African American identity. While at the end of the nineteenth century, African American women were consumed by a project that foregrounded the chastity and virtue of African American women, those concerns later broadened to include African American women's bodies and their fashion choices as a self-conscious comment on and critique of U.S. society within and outside of African American communities.

By and large, the women and children on this magazine's cover appear in highly posed tableaux reminiscent of the portraits by African American photographers like James Van der Zee. Some of the covers show models gazing solemnly out at readers, some show beaming women fishing in pristine white sailor suits, some show women in tennis or golf outfits, heads cocked to the side, lips slightly curved upward in a smile. Some of the covers image African American women who appear to have just finished a long afternoon of shopping, their neatly stacked boxes firmly gripped by well-proportioned hands, their eyes smiling beneath the brims of hats placed just so. One woman on a cover lights candles for her wayward spouse. The caption tells us of her hope that the light will guide her man home. Taken together, the covers tell a story about whom African American women could become in an urban arena; from the settings to the lighting to the positioning of the models and props, the covers make clear that there is a world of meaning to be found in fashion choices. All the women and girls portrayed are neat and well groomed. They would all, for example, have hair straightened and shaped into one of the many fashionable styles of the day. All their clothing and accessories were easily found for purchase inside the magazine.

While earlier magazines may have *told* African American women what they should be and how they should look, *Half-Century Magazine* would *show* readers what fashion could and did mean. Though presented in a publication most concerned with teaching certain classes of African American women how best to fit with their new surroundings, the meaning of race, class, and fashion as found on the cover would resonate with African American women across class lines.

For, example, the image in figure 12 appeared on the cover of the March 1917 issue of the magazine. To state it most simply, the editors chose to announce their March 1917 issue by portraying a "maid" wrapped in an American flag. It is a comment on the employment opportunities most readily available to African American women as they migrated to cities like Chicago, at the same time that it is a call to see the figure and very bodies of African American women as the bearers of cultural politic and deserving of broader access to U.S. citizenship ideals. In describing the reasons for running such a cover, the editor further complicates matters when she suggests that the image pictures the height of African American women's femininity. It is clear that much is expected of this image, and the fit between what is shown and what is written is not always easy or seamless.

In the short article explaining the purpose of the cover, we are told that the "Maid in America" is "[l]ovely to the eyes in symbol and in fact. Adorable in her maidenly purity, queenly in her grace, loyal in her pride." After going to some lengths to explain that the cover depicts a forgiving love and patriotism that is at variance with the "body politic who put 'Made in England,' 'Made in Germany,' and other slogans of hyphenate loyalty in front of '*Made in America*,'" the article says that the image "symbolizes the only citizenry within the confines of the American nation that is really and truly 'Made in America' in body and in spirit—the only loyal element having no hyphenate affiliations and sympathies—the only element displaying at all times, despite the most bitter discouragements and the most utter handicaps, an unswerving loyalty to the colors that give them so little consideration and protection in their national life" (15). What the article neglects to do is delve into the clearly significant spelling in the image's title. While the explanation would seem to suggest that "made" in America is the spelling under discussion, what appears is "maid."

12. "Maid in America," March 1917

Though this is not remarked upon, it is clear that more than just place of birth and citizenship are at issue for the magazine in this image.

The cover is a not so subtle reminder that for African American women in the first few decades of the twentieth century, "maid" was both their title and occupation, and one of the few employment opportunities available to them as they migrated to cities like Chicago, where this magazine was published. In some cities, as many as 90 percent of African American women were engaged in domestic service as day workers, washerwomen, or live-in servants. We are left to wonder whether the spelling in the image's title is a plea to remember that African American women are being denied access to jobs as anything other than maids in urban America.[14] This was true whether one dressed in the latest fashions or in a flag. The cover is just one of many that sought to link the social realities of African American women and young girls to fashion.

For example, on the November–December 1922 cover entitled "Her Choice," a young African American girl stares out at readers as she clutches a doll to her chest. If the reader looks closely, the doll is African American, and there is a white doll sitting discarded at her feet. The white doll is nude and the Black one, clutched to the chest of the African American child, is fully clothed in an outfit that closely resembles that of the child. More than three decades before Kenneth and Mamie Clark's doll study would be offered as social scientific evidence in the historic *Brown v. Board of Education* case, *Half-Century Magazine* visualized this same issue for its readers on its cover. However, unlike the evidence offered in that case almost thirty years later, the young African American girl pictured on this magazine's cover has already chosen to play with the African American doll. We are left to wonder if any part of the reason for her choice involves the unfashionable nature of the white doll.

Given the lack of images of African American women in the mainstream press, it is hard to imagine that those in this magazine would not have called out to potential readers from the newsstands, coffee tables, and beauty shops where the magazine would have been found. Unlike representations of fashionable African American women in earlier periods, these were not pictures of a particular woman who had accomplished something significant, but rather they represented the possibility of any woman occupying the same page. The chance to view African American women occupying public spaces, to read about African American female

13. "Her Choice," November–December 1922

heroines as they negotiated an urban environment that was new to many of the fictional characters, as well as to the stories' readers, quickly made the magazine a project different from those undertaken by previous publications.

One of the most notable aspects of the cover of the magazine is its use of anonymous models. The use of such models is significant in relation to fashion and urbanization because, in a visual sense, they set up an equation within which anonymity plus fashion, when combined with an urban environment, offer the possibility of standing out from the crowd. Indeed, on each of the covers, the scenes are structured in such a way that the clothes take precedence and draw the reader's eye. While we may not know the model's name or any particular accomplishments she has under her figurative belt, we cannot help but see that in a literal sense, it is her belt that makes her special.

WHAT THEY ARE WEARING

In addition to its editorials, articles, letters, and covers like those discussed here, *Half-Century Magazine* pioneered a fashion page that included photographs of African American models wearing "fashionable styles." Instead of members of the African American elite representing the majority of images of African American women thought to be worthy of representation, this century would bring nameless, anonymous women to the fore. They, not the elite, would come to represent the whole. These pages caused quite a stir. In March 1916, the month after the first "What They Are Wearing" column included African American models, the magazine received a number of letters that reported the sensation it was causing. While none specifically mention the long-standing practice of using lithographed images of white women in columns and magazines that focused on fashion (like *Ringwood's Journal*), many of the letter writers are quick to praise the new practice. One writer from Denison, Texas, said that seeing the column "was something swell and has caused the *Half-Century Magazine* to double its circulation here." Another added that the new column was "the best yet, it is a new thing under the sun. This feature (if continued) will be a drawing card. Think of it. We will know just how the 'togs' will suit our own. Colored faces looking out of Fashion Plates. Well!" (18).

At times the heading for the fashion models proclaimed the items to be "Pin Money Frocks," and at other times the outfits were labeled "Smart Fashions for Limited Incomes." This focus

14. "Smart fashions," *Half-Century Magazine,* 1917

on frugal fashion is underscored by the summaries of the outfits. Skirts are "inexpensive and appropriate for almost any kind of wear." A suit is "inexpensive and one of the latest fall models." Each page, whether discussing suits, hats, or skirts, touts the utility of each item. A suit may be described as "very appropriate for both fall and winter wear." Others are picked because "you will need just one such suit as this one which has a great deal more utility to recommend it" (September 1916, 7). As was true in a number of the magazine's editorials about fashion, the pages that most pointedly represented it would go to some lengths to make clear that looking good need not cost much money at all.

This focus on utility would hold true when the magazine featured other articles of clothing—hats, for example. In the February 1917 issue the fashion page featured a layout entitled "Hats

15. "Hats for early spring," *Half-Century Magazine*, 1917

for Early Spring." Here, along with the prices for each hat and a reminder that the *Half-Century Magazine* shopping service will happily purchase and send any of the above-pictured hats to any interested readers, the caption under each photograph makes a point of mentioning that the hats are appropriate for "dress wear as well as street wear." Again, the versatility, small expense, and appropriate nature of the items are foregrounded, as is the information that the clothes can be purchased for you no matter where in the United States you might live.

Finally, the women pictured on the pages of the magazine represent a variety of heights, skin colors, and weights. They offer wide-ranging options for identification on the part of the magazine's readers. As a result, the fashion pages of *Half-Century Magazine* became one of the first spaces in print media where dark skinned African American women could find role models they might wish to emulate.

THE STATUS OF FASHION

While in an earlier period, those who may not have thought that fashion mattered much were all but absent, by the twentieth century, it is clear that readers not accorded membership in the elite classes of African Americans were far less sure that clothing indicated class status, and, judging by the frequency with which writers in *Half-Century Magazine* mention their run ins with those who do not have a firm understanding of fashion, they are very much in evidence in urban areas.[15] Indeed, as late as the 1960s, African American women who had migrated from the rural South to the urban Midwest or North would reflect on the significance of fashion in their early days in cities beyond the South. Interviewed in a study about the experience of migration, Louise Dillard explained that while she liked the fashions in the city, she could not help but disapprove of the emphasis placed on clothing and looking good. "Down South, we could wear anything because folk didn't care and we only paid attention to how we looked at church, and that did not require much, just a decent suit and a couple of nice dresses, but no pressure, like up here, when folk think you ought to be dressed up just to go to the store."[16] But fashion, what fashion meant, and who was looking at whom had long been issues in urban African American communities across the United States. At the very least, this was a primary concern in magazines owned, written by, and read by African American women.

While at the end of the nineteenth century, fashion and clothing were primarily discussed as a means to erase the cultural memory of African American women's rape during the antebellum period, the first few decades of the twentieth century would bring more focus to how fashion marked both migratory and class status. In both centuries, fashion came to matter a great deal. Given the sentiments of Louise Dillard, it would continue to do so for some time to come.

5

No Place Like Home

Domesticity, Domestic Work, and Consumerism

> From such small beginnings, the Afro-American woman was compelled to construct a home. She who had been an outcast, the caprice of brutal power and passion, who had been educated to believe that morality was an echo, and womanly modesty a name; she who had seen father and brother and child torn from her and hurried away into everlasting separation—this creature was born to life in an hour and expected to create a home.
>
> —*Victoria Earle Matthews, 1897*

AT the turn of the twentieth century, the possibility of African American women creating a home environment considered culturally acceptable, if not redemptive, was most often connected to their escaping a history of enslavement and to an all-consuming search for a future defined by morality, virtue, and refinement. That women so newly removed from slavery's reach should be expected to understand and embrace the dominant definition of home and domesticity caused many quite a bit of consternation. Such concerns, expressed as everything from constructive criticism to outright ridicule, occupied no small amount of space in African American women's magazines at the time. Such publications were a key site for teaching African American women how to embody mainstream discourses surrounding femininity, womanhood, and cultural manifestations of a domestic ideal. In these magazines, and specifically different from the representation of domesticity for white women, generational and class dynamics played key roles in how the ideal was discussed, deployed, and understood. *Ringwood's Journal,* for example, offered young working-class women and girls the vision of soul-deadening domestic work as the primary possibility for a modern relationship to domesticity. The connection between domesticity and domestic work was buttressed by a logic that privileged "home" as the most desirable place for a woman; it mattered little if that home was her own, or that of her white employer.

Similar discourses were found in turn-of-the-century novels, newspaper articles, magazine columns, and etiquette manuals. However, because elite groups of African American female intellectuals, writers, activists, and businesspeople were committed to a portrayal of domestic labor as a noble pursuit essential for racial uplift, they went to great lengths to craft a narrative that included African American women from different class positions. From working-class women who were portrayed as too ignorant or lazy to embrace the opportunity to work as domestics, to those of the elite who were chastised for allowing their love of adornment and leisure to interfere with their work in the home, African American women were urged to embrace, by any means at their disposal, mainstream cultural ideals that related home and domesticity to moral fortitude and character development.[1] Surprisingly, then, by the 1920s domesticity would no longer denote moral fortitude but primarily become an opportunity for product consumption. *Half-Century Magazine,* for example, argued that life as either a paid or unpaid domestic worker would certainly not be so bad if one but knew how to identify and purchase the cookware, food, and products for the home considered modern and glamorous. Making the right choices would by extension make the shopper modern and glamorous as well. Accordingly, as the twentieth century unfolded, the rhetoric of domestic work and domesticity in relation to home become a narrative primarily advocating the purchase and consumption of products as a way of symbolizing domesticity, modernity, and urbanization.

If in these same magazines, fashion came to represent a means to combat an undesirable past with its assumptions about African American female morality and virtue, discussions of home and its significance became a compass that directed readers toward a future free from such concerns. Unlike the ways in which a similar rhetoric of consumption and its relationship to modernity was crafted to address middle-class white readers of mainstream women's magazines, in African American women's magazines, the past, slavery, sexuality, and the need to overcome the resulting historical stain provided a complex backdrop for understanding the meaning of and changes in discussions around the relationships between domesticity, modernity, and shopping.

Home and Turn-of-the-Century American Culture in Black and White

In relation to white American culture and the publications aimed at a white female readership, the central tenets of a domestic ideology that connected home to morality and defined it as a particularly female space had been developing in fiction and nonfiction since the 1830s. It was reiterated most fully in the 1870s when Catharine Beecher and Harriet Beecher Stowe published *The American Woman's Home,* the text that became the bible of the domestic science movement. In the ideology of domestic science, the home and domesticity were connected to character, virtue, and morality and depended on historically specific ideas on housekeeping and the organization of domestic space.[2] The power to provide household moral instruction was touted as the true reward for embracing the ideology and the overwhelming amount of labor that enacting such an ideal entailed, and Marilyn Ferris Motz has noted that in nineteenth-century culture, "the atmosphere of the home was seen as having an almost mystical effect on its inhabitants determining their moral standards, happiness, and success in the outside world."[3]

As far as women like Victoria Earle Matthews were concerned, most African American women faced a daunting challenge in their ability to understand either the significance or the ideological

power of home and domesticity. It was up to those who did understand to guide their less informed sisters along the proper, if at
times twisted and convoluted, ideological paths.[4] They used African American women's magazines, as well as other cultural productions, to advance their cause.

In the tableau represented in figure 16, viewers are invited into
what in 1904 was described as a "modern" African American
home. We see three generations of an African American family
spending the evening in each other's company. A handsome father
attired in evening wear playfully throws his young son in the air;
a slim mother wearing a formal gown plays the piano, while her
small daughter looks on appreciatively. A grandfather decked out
in a tuxedo chuckles as he bounces his grandson on his knee,
while a modestly garbed grandmother studiously reads nearby.
The image shows viewers that in a "modern" middle-class African American home the children are clean, neatly attired, and well
looked after; the women are modestly and fashionably dressed;
the men are elegantly attired, happy, and seemingly content; the
surroundings are orderly and clean. It is an image of domesticity
that presents family togetherness as a key to prosperity, content-
ment, and, perhaps most importantly, morality. Though representing an African American household, it would have been easily
recognizable to a white woman at the turn of the twentieth century as an image to which mainstream magazines and publications urged her to aspire in her own home.

For African Americans, this image represented what many
believed was a direct though unexplored road to racial uplift,
cultural acceptance, and social advancement. The role of the
African American female elite in this effort is key. As Amy Wolf
has rightly noted, home decoration in particular and domestic
space in general attained crucial significance for the African
American middle classes. Wolf argues that "although housekeeping could be confining as well as liberating, in marked contrast
to the position of African American women during slavery,
housekeeping allowed black women increased opportunities for
self-definition, for claiming not only space but self-hood. Black

16. A modern African American home

women authors especially could use domestic settings as a vehicle for addressing issues of self-articulation, claiming a distinctly female space, and emphasizing the power for political change that they saw inherent in that space." Unlike white women's embrace of the domestic ideal, because African American women were only a generation removed from slavery "with its shadow still a powerful collective memory, the black woman's control over the domestic sphere represents a power previously only granted to white women or freed blacks."[5] It is this trust in the emancipatory power and singular significance of home for previously enslaved African American women that accounts for the frequency with which such narratives appeared in the magazines they wrote and edited.

In the November–December 1923 issue of *Half-Century Magazine,* a serialized story entitled "Gains for Losses" is advertised by telling readers that they should read the story to find how a young woman named Mary "finds glory and the world's applause a poor substitute for the joys of home-making."[6] The story's protagonist, Mary Hampton, is an orphan who at the age of fourteen was adopted by an African American family in a town merely referred to as Carterville.[7] Mary soon finds that her new parents are less interested in providing her with a home than in having unpaid domestic labor in theirs. Not only does Mary do all of the cooking and cleaning for her new mother and father (the Barbees) and their five children, but also she proves herself to be a gifted and "cheerful" seamstress. Additionally, she discovers a talent for auto mechanics and quickly becomes one of the most sought-after mechanics in her adopted father's garage. However, the other young people in the town primarily see her as little more than a servant and are disinclined to socialize with her. As a result, there is no possibility of her secret crush on the Barbees' oldest son, Jack, ever amounting to anything, and she spends most of her time alone and miserable. While she possesses the necessary skills to become a successful homemaker, she lacks the husband, background, and social standing that would complete the package.

To literally make a long story short (the story is serialized over three issues), Mary's skill as a mechanic serves her well when she helps a wealthy stranger fix his car. It has broken down and left him stranded. In return, upon discovering that it is Mary's eighteenth birthday, he gives her two hundred dollars and a ride to Cleveland, Ohio. While in Cleveland, she discovers that she has quite a bit of singing talent and a successful career follows. Six years later, her newfound celebrity occasions her return to Carterville, where Jack, who attends her concert, immediately dumps his current girlfriend and declares himself in love with Mary. In short order, Mary chooses to leave her flashy career to get to work bearing and raising their children.

This story serves as a synopsis of the dominant narrative surrounding the meaning of home in both U.S. culture and African

American women's magazines. While single African American women often needed to work outside the home to support themselves (in white women's magazine fiction, work is usually optional and pursued only for enjoyment), frequently fictional stories and advice columns in such magazines center on correcting the assumption that a career or life outside the domestic sphere can bring personal happiness and fulfillment. Consistently, any African American women contemplating such a life are portrayed as misguided. By the end of the stories, they eagerly leave the world of paid labor to become wives. Accordingly, at the end of this story, Mary's long-sought-after beau looks at her and says, "I've no doubt that some day you'll climb dizzying heights of success; you may win laurels before crowned heads, but when I heard you sing 'Po' Li'l Lamb,' I could not help thinking how much lovelier you'd look crooning to a little lamb of your own" (ibid.). Upon hearing these words, Mary immediately begins to cry and realizes that a home of her own is all she really ever wanted (22). In short, Mary embodies the sentimental ideal popular in nineteenth- and early-twentieth-century fiction and ever-present in works aimed at both African American and white female readers of fiction.

In explaining the difference race makes in such stories, Claudia Tate has argued that while the traditional sentimental plot like that in "Gains for Losses" is in one instance conservative, when African American women writers use it, it often becomes a subversive device that illustrates a desire for political and cultural agency. Tate goes on to suggest that one traditional discourse that black women novelists of the turn of the century challenge is the idea that black women are "lacking virtue, are somehow controlled solely by their passions." By presenting "a heroine who is an exemplar of feminine purity, piety, and the work ethic," as well as by outlining "a plot that confirms bourgeois social objectives of domesticity and respectability," these writers "posit an alternative that espouses the virtue and purity previously associated only with white women."[8] Certainly this paradigm helps explain Mary, who begins the story a penniless orphan but ends it having both attained a successful career and used her knowledge of mechanics to effect a change in her life. If the meaning of race changes the understanding of mainstream literary forms within the sentimental ideal, a focus on class and generation within ideologies of race troubles the meaning even more.

For members of the African American intellectual elite, home and domesticity were always about far more than merely finding a soul mate, or fulfilling a long-held desire for children. At the turn of the nineteenth century, and against the backdrop of mainstream cultural views of African Americans as far outside the ideological mainstream, marriage, children, and an acceptable home equaled refinement and character. Booker T. Washington, for example, in a 1902 magazine article entitled "Negro Homes," opens the essay by noting: "I do not believe it is possible for any one to judge very thoroughly of the life of any individual or race unless he gets into the homes."[9] In a similar article in *The Colored American Magazine* from 1905, Edna Wheeler Wilcox declares in "On the Making of Homes" that "at the present era, I would say that a higher ideal of the home, and of what is demanded of those who have received a certain amount of education in their attitude toward that home, is important for the colored race to attain." Wilcox ends by surmising that "the home . . . marks the progress of any race from the crude to the civilized state."[10]

While the African American intellectual elite used various pulpits and publications to expound upon their views of home and domesticity, African American culture more broadly defined was overrun with such types of discussions. Among the most persistent purveyors were conduct or etiquette books. For example, *Golden Thoughts on Chastity and Procreation including Heredity, Prenatal Influences, Etc., Etc.,* by Professor and Mrs. J. W. Gibson, includes the illustration that began this chapter with an image of what they term "a modern home." That publication included more than twenty

"representative" images, like that pictured in figure 17, that would show readers the particulars of dress, behavior, and expectation in African American homes. All would prominently feature African American women as central to African American homes in any number of highly posed settings.

The subtitle of the Gibsons' manual is "Sensible Hints and Wholesome Advice for Maiden and Young Man, Wife and Husband, Mother and Father," and the introduction explains that such images represent the "inside home life of fully one-third of the ten million colored Americans." They are described as telling

17. "Evening Prayer"

the story of a new aristocracy, a people powerful in strength, morals, culture, wealth, and refinement." On the one hand, the book is written for African Americans to tell them how to "perfect themselves in all things social, economical, physical, political, and financial," and on the other hand, it "proves to those who are inclined to think otherwise that some good thing can come out of Ethiopia."[11] Significantly, if there is a problem in the African American home, it is usually traced back to the absence of a mother fully conscious of her responsibilities or the consequences of her choices relative to the home.

In this guide, the home was singled out as the locus for crime and degeneracy, if not properly maintained and structured. Indeed, to save later generations, readers are beseeched to follow specific courses of action. The results of not following the offered advice were, the argument went, frightening to the African American race as a whole. As illustrated by figures 18 and 19, taken from *Golden Thoughts,* the price for doing any less than that represented in the publication was to doom one's offspring (and by extension the African American race) to lives of crime and overall degeneracy.

The children of the "poor and uneducated" are represented as dirty, unhappy, and poorly groomed. Unlike the progeny of "pure and educated parents," the text describes them as predisposed to criminal delinquency from the moment of conception. Their lives and futures are doomed as a result of inattentiveness to home life, and often as a result of misguided attempts on the part of their mothers to seek employment outside the domestic sphere. Economics, racism, and structured inequality were all pushed aside as rationales for African American poverty and financial inequality in favor of those that located the home (and most often African American women) as the locus of the problem. However, given that so much in U.S. culture argued against the possibility of African Americans having the ability to curb a biological disposition toward criminal behavior, the fact that such productions portrayed a group of African Americans who had, through the benefit of proper domestic instruction, risen beyond their sup-

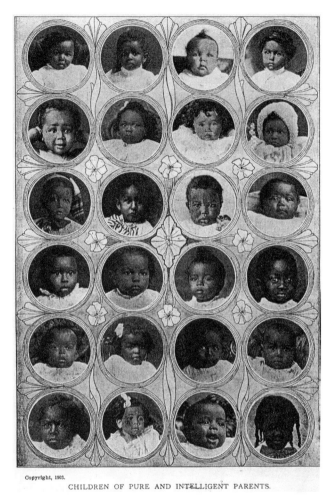

CHILDREN OF PURE AND INTELLIGENT PARENTS.

18. "Children of pure and intelligent parents"

posed station in life was notable indeed. It was a testament to the efficacy of the rhetoric of home and domesticity.

This focus on the home, morality, decency, and degeneracy would take, in African American society and culture at large, a curious shape in relation to young African American women. While fictional and other cultural narratives crafted by African American women in the late nineteenth and early twentieth centuries posited marriage as the primary means of achieving a

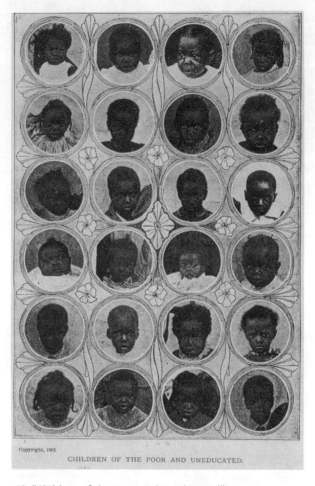

Copyright, 1903.

CHILDREN OF THE POOR AND UNEDUCATED.

19. "Children of the poor and uneducated"

desired relationship to domesticity and of uplifting an entire race, elsewhere in African American women's magazines, engaging in domestic work for pay was advocated just as vigorously. What bears further investigation is how such a construct could come to mean that young African American women should so crave the experience of domesticity that they would willingly and happily choose to work as servants in the homes of white women. Calls for a utopian home existed alongside calls for young African

American women to work as domestics in the homes of whites, if they could not create idealized domestic spaces for themselves.

GENDER, GENERATION, AND DOMESTIC WORK

In the "Talks about Women" column of the April 1911 issue of the *Crisis*, Mrs. John E. Millholland, while discussing the benefits of training African American women for domestic work, explained that "when the advantages of domestic work are considered, the wonder is that more American women do not properly equip themselves for such a life." The writer, after urging any of her readers who are young, African American, and unemployed to consider professional training that will help them learn the proper attitudes and behaviors that go along with becoming a modern domestic, concludes that we can only hope "our young women— colored and white—will feel that if they have a taste for domestic service they may go into it without thinking, as they do now, that they are losing their social standing amongst their own set" (23).

The concern over young African American women not choosing domestic work as a career was echoed in the women's column from the *New York Age* in July 1911. In this instance, the writer, after pointing out that ten thousand white girls have left the domestic trade in New York and suggesting that this turn of events means those jobs are just waiting for African American women who may want them, complains that young African American women have a bad habit of leaving these types of jobs before they are properly completed, or refusing to do this type of work at all. She adds that Hampton and Tuskegee offer wonderful courses in domestic science and urges mothers to prevail upon their daughters to take advantage of them as "the first order of domestic training for young girls is to help their mothers in the home" (12).

The consistent pressure young African American women faced as to where and for whom they would work was applied by an older generation deeply anxious about the relationship of African American women to modernity, the vice associated with the city, and the contemporary place of the Victorian sensibilities with which they had been engrained when they had been young themselves. Those who espoused the glories of domestic work were attempting to contain, control, and shape the behavior of young African American women to protect them from a slew of modern vices and to discourage negative behaviors in which the older generation believed the younger wished to engage. As one mother wrote to Nannie Burroughs when explaining her reasons for sending her thirteen-year-old daughter to Burroughs's National Training School for Women and Girls, her daughter "wanted to be too modern for my taste."[12]

While these concerns and tensions were most forcefully expressed during the first few decades of the twentieth century, the dress rehearsal for what would become a fully staged drama shaped up much earlier in the pages of magazines aimed at an African American female audience. *Ringwood's Journal* helps to chart the complex web of expectations African American women had of each other across boundaries of age, location, and class and centers specifically on the place of young African American women in relation to the rhetoric of home and domesticity. Given that during the antebellum period and after, domestic work such as the type advocated in the magazine was discussed as one of the prime opportunities for sexual violation, it is surprising that in an effort to control the bodies and identities of young women at the turn of the century, their mothers and grandmothers would urge them to take up these occupations. Given the economic and social realities of the time, and the fact that white employers barred African American women from other types of occupations, domestic service came to be seen and discussed as symbolic of racial oppression. At the same time, elite groups of African American women argued that if household labor was professionalized and rationalized, African American women would be viewed as workers, rather than as sexual objects.

In a particularly telling example of the larger political project of connecting home, urbanization, domestic work, and sexual violation, one of editors of *Ringwood's Afro-American Journal of*

Fashion, Victoria Earle Matthews, in 1897 founded the White Rose Mission and Traveler's Aid Society in New York City. Its purpose was to establish and maintain "a Christian, non-sectarian Home for Colored Girls and Women, where they may be trained in the principles of practical self-help and right living," and to "protect self-supporting Colored girls and direct and help them amid the dangers and temptations of New York City."[13] Matthews and her agents met the arriving trains and buses full of African American women migrating to the urban North from the South in order prevent such women from being approached and harassed by men bent on luring them into a life of prostitution and sexual service, or into signing employment contracts that would bind them to years of unpaid labor. Because it was common practice for employment agents to go into the rural districts of the South and convince young women to sign binding contracts in exchange for the money to migrate, many of those who disembarked for what they hoped would be a new life found that they were at the mercy of the agencies that had financed the trip. Matthews intervened and gave such women a place to live, along with the skills needed to refine their domestic service skills (sewing, cooking, and housekeeping courses were offered). As a result, home as related to refinement and respectability and defined through paid domestic work took center stage in a dialogue between African American women of differing class and generational backgrounds at the turn of the century and in the pages of *Ringwood's Afro-American Journal of Fashion.*

The character of young African American girls is consistently called into question and policed within the pages of *Ringwood's Afro-American Journal of Fashion.* Writing in the "Mother's Corner" column of the May–June 1893 issue, Sarah G. Jones goes so far as to suggest that, "among all people," young girls are most in need of "that which they are least anxious to embrace; the opportunities which are presented for improvement." They are "ignorant," "being almost a separate people, with no sympathies in common with the cultured" (79). In another article from the same issue, a writer notes: "It is a difficult matter for young women who are competent to secure employment as teachers, and they consider many of the occupations usually engaged in by women as menial and beneath their dignity . . . a special stress must be laid upon the dignity of labor." The writer goes on to assure mothers of such girls that this attitude will change once the girls are taught that "able men and women have devoted the greater part of their lives to reducing cooking and housekeeping to a science" (81).

While it is a fairly simple matter to ascertain the beliefs an older generation of African American women held about its daughters and granddaughters as pertains to domestic work, we have precious little information about how young African American women responded. Indeed, there is only one article in *Ringwood's Journal* that allows a voice from that group to be heard. In an 1893 column entitled "Talk to Our Girls," the editor tells readers that she has received a number of letters from young African American women who complain that their elders should not tell them to become and enjoy being domestics. We are told that this young writer asserts that her generation views this type of work with trepidation and questions their ability to ever be considered truly feminine if forced to continue in this type of employment. While raising the banner of femininity would, given the publication's overwhelming concern with the topic, seem to be a savvy move on the part of the unnamed letter writer, she learned that this was one instance in which appealing to and for refinement would be a less than successful strategy. The column's editor, Susie I. Lankford Shorter, responds: "There is no good reason why a woman should cease to be feminine because she is compelled to work, but it too often happens that the girls who are forced to earn their own living become imbued with a spirit of independence and bravado" (79). Shorter, after assuring readers that a woman's duty is in the home (either her own or her employer's), goes on to complain that domestic work is not the problem, but rather the belief on the part of the young that wage work entitles one to a degree of independence from husbands and parents. As Shorter's response makes evident, it was no easy thing to advocate wage earning and at the same time argue that such earners should continue to assume a posture of dependence and deference. Indeed, it was slippery terrain.

In many urban areas, domestic work was one of the few occupations readily available to African American women, who often continued to work outside of the home even after marriage. At the turn of the century, between 50 and 60 percent of African American women remained in the workforce after they were married, with the numbers reaching even higher in some locales. In addition, given that migration to the east coast of the United States was overwhelmingly female (migration to the West was overwhelmingly male), marriage and stay-at-home domesticity were far removed from the lived realities of a majority of African American women.[14] While a handful could perhaps find work in industry or retail employment, and others were able to support themselves as seamstresses, or possibly as schoolteachers or hairdressers, the vast majority had no choice but to seek work in domestic service. Within that context, it is not at all surprising that a turn-of-the-century magazine would urge its African American female readers to set their sights on domestic work as a career. It is not that they were urged to work as domestics that I find notable, but rather the ways in which the publication chose to address its young female readers on the subject.

The articles in *Ringwood's Journal* about domestic work and about the character of young African American women neatly sum up one strand of the overarching ideological and cultural work of discourses of domesticity aimed at African American women at the turn of the century. Unlike the images that would circulate in the "race movies" of Oscar Micheaux and others in the early 1920s (which generally portrayed idealized versions of African American female domesticity), the discourses in African American women's magazines at the end of the nineteenth century urged young African American women to enter the world of wage labor as domestic servants and to do so eagerly and cheerfully. They further suggested that there was little difference between domestic work for pay and that performed within the confines of marriage and motherhood. At the same time, the journal expounded on the glories of a domesticity that is primarily defined as marriage and stay-at-home motherhood. That such differing positions could result in an uneasy détente is due in no small part to dynamics of class and generation operating at the end of that century. Many of the writers and editors for the magazine subscribed to an elitist ideology that predicated cultural and societal acceptance on specific manners, morals, and behaviors. For African American women who embraced the ideology of domesticity, such acceptance was constituted by admission into both a respectably elite African American community and a larger white society. In either space, young readers were urged to constantly police their behavior, or to risk humiliation and rejection for themselves, for their undeserving families, and finally for the African American race as an undifferentiated whole.

This formulation of domestic work and its relation to femininity and womanhood is significantly different from that found in turn-of-the-century women's magazines for either urban middle-class or rural white women. For example, *Ladies' World,* edited by Frances E. Fryatt and published between 1890 and 1915, was aimed at convincing rural women that it was possible for them to enter a gender-based modernity and foster class mobility by having access to the same goods and products heavily marketed to middle-class women. In order to earn money for the purchase of these products, the white rural woman was told to start a business she could conduct from home that would capitalize on work in which she was already engaged, such as selling eggs, growing berries, bartering sewing for labor, or knitting. The caveat was that the work had to be performed within the home and the money had to be spent to better that environment. Unlike the rhetoric of work in *Ringwood's Journal,* it was never suggested that women should work to support themselves or their families. While *Ladies' World* encouraged traditionally feminine forms of labor, none of the articles, stories, or editorials in white women's magazines ever entertained the notion that a rural white housewife should enter domestic service in anyone else's home.[15]

In comparison, *Ladies' Home Journal,* aimed primarily at a middle-class white female reading public, accused married women who contemplated working in order to hire domestic help of shirking their more important responsibilities to their husbands and children. In an 1893 editorial, one writer complained: "Lately there has been a great deal of fretful impatient, womanly writing, about the degrading, depressing influence of household work; and it has been urged that it is better for wives and mothers to write or sew, or do any kind of mental work, in order to make money to relieve themselves of the duties of cooking and nursing. Women who have this idea ought never to have become wives, and they ought never, never, never to have become mothers."[16]

For the turn-of-the-century readers of *Ladies' Home Journal,* wage earning is disparaged as an excuse to hire domestic help in order to escape the womanly duties of cooking and nursing. Wage earning, while at least in some situations considered acceptable for rural white women, is flatly forbidden for middle-class white women who are also wives and mothers. Clearly, any number of white rural women worked to support themselves and their families instead of just to beautify their homes. There were also working-class women who earned wages in factories and other types of clerical and service industries. Of course, there were middle-class women who, if they could afford it, continued to employ domestics. Pronouncements such as those found in the magazines spoke of an exaggerated ideal that had little relationship to the realities of white women's lives.

However, the vast majority of African American women who worked outside the home were domestic servants. In *Ringwood's Journal,* domestic work, sewing, and prostitution were among the few options ever discussed for uneducated African American women (although, of course, prostitution is condemned). Negotiating such narrow career options must surely have been uppermost in the minds of young African American women, and a magazine such as *Ringwood's Journal* would have been one place they could turn for advice. To fit themselves into rigid late-nineteenth-century definitions of femininity and womanhood, readers of African American women's magazines like *Ringwood's Journal* were urged to find their highest, truest, most rewarding work inside a home and in relation to the care of others—especially children. The magazine, then, struggled to reinscribe the practice within a discourse of domesticity that argued for the nobility of work as a domestic servant outside the home.

In relation to cultural assertions about home and the significance of home for African Americans in general, it becomes clear that while the rationale for urging young African American women to cheerfully embrace domestic work may be a bitter pill for a twenty-first-century reader to swallow, it was part of a larger political project that foregrounded the uplift of African Americans as a whole. Significantly, the rhetoric and strategy for achieving the uplift of African Americans would shift again in the first few decades of the twentieth century in the pages of *Half-Century Magazine* and become much more democratic in terms of who could participate in the ideal of domesticity.

FROM CHARACTER TO CONSUMPTION

Half-Century Magazine showed its readers how to maintain and live in a home successfully and argued that the purchase and consumption of the proper products would lead to societal acceptance and racial uplift. This new focus on product consumption, while a radical shift in narratives of home in African American magazines, was not out of step with larger developments in U.S. consumer culture. The period from 1880 to 1930 was marked by several crucial developments that firmly established modern America's capitalist consumer culture. These developments included the concentration and centralization of capital, the rise of mass production and national distribution, the emergence of scientific management, and the decrease in the number of craft communities. Among other changes in their lives, as African American women moved to cities, they often lost the means to manufacture many standard provisions and, as a result, were forced to become much more reliant on manufactured products. While non-mail-

NO PLACE LIKE HOME   109

order advertisers of national brand products were reluctant (if not downright resistant) to place advertisements in African American newspapers and periodicals until *Ebony* magazine began publication in 1945, African American companies and service providers advertised in African American women's magazines on a regular basis. These companies provided an entree for African American women into a mass-market economy, and working-class African American women were the primary shoppers in their communities and families.

Unlike many ethnic communities and workers, African Americans did not reject the rise of commercial insurance, chain stores, credit, or standard brands. At least in Chicago and New York, African American receptivity to mass culture grew in response to increasing calls for a separate Black economy. At the center of the separate African American economy stood race business. Pastors and newspaper articles told African American consumers that when they patronized Black businesses they bought jobs, entrepreneurship, and independence along with goods and services. African American consumer dollars supported all kinds of businesses by the twenties, but benefited most those whose products, services, or companies were geared solely to African American needs. One of these businesses was Anthony Overton's Hygienic Manufacturing Company. It was connected with and advertised heavily in *Half-Century Magazine*.

Anthony Overton was born a slave in Monroe, Louisiana. After attending the University of Kansas, he became a lawyer and municipal judge. With $1,960 and two employees, he began his business career in Kansas City in 1898 by manufacturing baking powder. After a few years of limited success, he moved to Chicago in 1911 and added a cosmetics line. By 1915, his company was capitalized at over $260,000 and had thirty-two employees.[17] Overton, like other African American entrepreneurs at the time, attempted to capitalize on the success enjoyed by Madam C. J. Walker in serving the beauty and health needs of African American women. His High Brown Face Powder met with success similar to, if not as dramatic as, that of Walker's products, and he built a factory in Chicago and funded *Half-Century Magazine* to advertise his products. Overton's firm manufactured more than half of the products advertised in that publication. As a result, the relationship between product consumption and prescriptive advice about the home is tightly drawn.

For example, in a September 1916 column titled "The Care of the Hair," the author states that "modern specialists" have discovered that washing the hair once a month or every six weeks is "no less unhygienic than the 'Saturday Night' bath" (11). The column ends with instructions to the reader on the way to use shampoo and is followed by a full-page advertisement for such products manufactured by the Overton Company. The step-by-step guide to hair washing is coupled with an article in the Domestic Science column entitled "What to Eat and How to Cook It" that instructs African American women on the procedure for selecting beef from the butcher (11). Similar to the article on hair washing, it offers a step-by-step guide to handling meat once it is home. Following these admonishments are several recipes for cooking the steak, complete with the brand-name ingredients one should use for seasoning.

Half-Century Magazine's women readers were advised on how to clean carpets and curtains, how to organize kitchen utensils, how old newspapers could be used, how to mend a screen, and how to remove varnish from furniture. Home and the duties of a woman in the home came to be associated with the purchase and preparation of products, as opposed to associated with the roles of wife and mother primarily responsible for moral instruction. Things, not feelings, duty, or behavior, became far more important in the twentieth century, as the prescriptive emphasis in African American women magazines shifted from values to valuables.

In addition to pointing African American women toward the most acceptable products for keeping a home running smoothly, the magazine included columns for women concerned with "proper" etiquette when "coming to call" on friends and acquaintances, as well as procedures for planning large weddings and hiring competent "help." By including such radically different columns, the editors and writers cater to different class positions in the African American female community. It is difficult to believe that the women who are interested in the finer points of etiquette such as what to wear, what times to call, what type of calling cards to have printed up, and what food to serve guests (all, by the way, activities that would have required the purchase of goods) were the same women who had no idea what a stove was or how to shampoo their hair. It would appear that the magazine spoke in one voice to its elite readers who knew the place and importance of products in their lives, and in another to those whom they believed needed this type of indoctrination to life in the North. Within a few decades, the significance and meaning of a modern home for African American women would, depending on the class and age of the audience addressed, make a meandering journey from a primary association with domesticity, to an espousal of the glories of paid domestic work in the homes of whites, to a representation of home as most significant in relation to product consumption. At different times, all three were described as the most modern and therefore significant relationship to the construct of home for African American women. The home and its delineation of class identity was an ever-present, though often changing, construct in publications aimed at an African American female readership.

At the turn of the twentieth century, African American magazine culture was rife with voices attempting to attract the attention of African American women migrating from rural areas to cities and provide them advice about the home. Among the most insistent, and at times shrill, were those belonging to African American women themselves, who raised their voices in the hopes of convincing, cajoling, and coercing young women into domestic work as a career choice. African American women's full-throated embrace of domesticity as an act of what Claudia Tate has argued was the manifestation of "political desire" formed the basis for urging young, urban African American women cheerfully to accept such work as their most productive relationship to ideals of domesticity.[18]

By the 1920s, modernity was no longer defined as the desire for a home and family, or even as providing care for a white family's home. The cleaning up of dirt would no longer form the basis for an opportunity to prove virtue, modesty, and character. Moral instruction would no longer form the unexamined basis for arguments positing the centrality of homes. Instead, glamour—as defined by the decoration of the home, as well as the home-maker—would come to dominate discussions of home and its significance for African American women. Between 1920 and 1950, the meanings of and narratives about sexual desire and domesticity, in the cultural context of African American's magazines and in relation to the commodification of urban African American female desire, would continue to dominate the editorial concerns of African American women's magazines.

6

Urban Confessions and Tan Fantasies

The Commodification of Marriage and Sexual Desire in African American Magazine Fiction

We can't get too many short stories. So let them come fast and thick.
. . . We aim to please the women and make *Half-Century* popular.
We do not want philosophy, science, sociology, and eloquence—we
editors have plenty of that ourselves. Our people—tired at the end
of the day's work—have no time to consume solid literary stuff.
They want diversion and recreation, and will read anything stimu-
lating and refreshing. They will read light, airy fiction—full of snap,
pep and go. Don't go into the church-house for all your plots.

— Half-Century Magazine, *February 1916*

Dear Editor: I've been reading confession magazines since I was 16
and I guess my life wouldn't be the same without them. They're the
most enjoyable minutes of the day for me. For a long time I've
thought that it would be wonderful if there would be a Colored
magazine of this kind and just when I about gave up hope, I noticed
where *Ebony* was bringing out one. . . . Congratulations to you for
giving the public, especially the Colored woman magazine reader
what she's always wanted.

— *Mattie Johnson*, Tan Confessions, *December 1950*

THE development of urban short fiction as a staple in *Half-Century Magazine* occurred quite rapidly. By February of 1917, the publication told readers it aimed to be "the greatest Colored short-story magazine in the world." In providing direction to budding writers and storytellers interested in having their work published in the magazine, the editors would, as the opening epigraph makes clear, publish only that which they deemed sensational, easy to understand, and, above all, entertaining. Specifically, they told prospective writers, "we want stories that are easily digested, stories with plenty of action—full of romance, love, and sentiment, stories in which the superficial qualities are cultivated—like fluency and wit, and the glamour of money, and a few touches of pathos and purity and no difficulties for the understanding."[1] The stories the editors chose for publication overwhelmingly focused on the difficulties of finding and maintaining urban love relationships and centered on women who were attempting to grow, change, and fully inhabit the cities to which they had recently moved. As the characters define themselves, they desire the opportunity to shop, dress, entertain themselves, and explore freely without the sanction of male approval or support. At the same time, in what was undoubtedly an acknowledgment of the function of romance stories, as well as of the high numbers of unmarried African American women flocking to urban areas, many of the stories end with a happy marriage.

In the 1920s and in keeping with understandings of the most effective ways of addressing racial inequalities, fictional stories about African American women in relation to urbanization and migration portrayed all roads as leading "home." Through the espousal of a turn-of-the-century political strategy highlighting manners, morals, refinement, and respectability, the stories made clear that success in such arenas would not only guarantee matrimonial bliss, but also assure the uplift and advancement of African Americans as a whole. Significantly, while experimentation with urban forms of entertainment defined the early portions of the stories, the female protagonists, once married, replaced their interest in their urban environments with a focus on building an ideal domestic environment. Within this context, the consumption of products was discussed as helping to make a house a happy home, but the publication made clear that consumption was ultimately less important than obtaining the cultural respectability that a stable and committed marriage would provide.

By the 1950s, stories of urban love and marriage took a decidedly different turn. In the pages of *Tan Confessions*, African American women were represented as damaged by urbanization and overly sexualized. They were also portrayed, above all else, as ardent consumers. In this publication, the point of getting or staying married was to ensure access to a husband's earnings in order to participate in the culture of consumption. It was only within the confines of committed domesticity, readers were told, that they would ever be able to enjoy the full privileges of product consumption and find sexual satisfaction and personal happiness. While all roads would once again lead to marriage, the purchase and consumption of products would be offered in this later period as the primary reason to participate in the institution.

In keeping with a burgeoning post–World War II social strategy to promote racial progress for African Americans, *Tan Confessions* equated racial success and advancement with the possession of material goods. The purchase of such products was positioned as an instrument of aggression, or a weapon, in the overall struggle for racial equality.[2] Toward that end, *Tan Confessions* portrayed African American female sexual desire as a commodity worthy of consumer purchase and, at the same time, as currency capable of purchasing male attention, economic privilege, and domestic stability. In short, African American women were both consumed and urged to become consumers.

MARRIAGE, URBAN SPACE, AND TURN-OF-THE-CENTURY WRITING

While the first few issues of *Half-Century Magazine* included short stories that focused on African American men who suffered injustice at the hands of southern or rural whites,[3] by March

1917, the magazine featured at least three short stories written by African American women with African American female protagonists. One of the first such short stories was written by a woman who became a frequent contributor. Her name was Bettie Mason, and her first story for *Half-Century Magazine*, in the March 1917 issue, was entitled "Did He Marry Clara James?" In this story, a young, aspiring, but as yet unpublished writer named Cameron Frank has recently moved to Chicago to try and make a name for himself as an author. He takes up residence in a rooming house, where he is happy to find that no women are allowed as renters. It would appear that his feelings about women have to do with his social awkwardness, as the story tells us that despite the fact that on a "damp, drizzly Sunday in March, too disagreeable for walking, and yet rather lonesome at home with no one to talk to," he chooses to stay in his room reading as opposed to making an effort to befriend the landlady's daughter. He feels that "she was too frightfully enthusiastic over everything" and so chooses to stay in his room (5).

Cameron's isolation is soon shattered, and his social skills are challenged, when the landlady rents a room to a young woman named Clara James. She is a writer who spends most of her time in her room typing her new novel, hand washing and hanging her intimate apparel out to dry, and singing quietly to herself. In short order, Cameron finds himself intrigued by his fellow author. His attraction is heightened when:

> A few evenings later, he sauntered into his favorite restaurant. She was there. She smiled graciously. A sudden impulse, born of sheer loneliness, made Cameron walk over and seat himself at her table. To his surprise he found her interesting. More than that, she wore very good clothes. It made Cameron wonder— the constant writing late at night; the costly clothes; the refinement. Perhaps, after all, fortune had decided in his favor. Gradually, cautiously, he turned the conversation to books and their authors. They began to discuss colored writers. (5)

In the course of the meal he soon unintentionally insults her. He mistakes her hesitancy about discussing a certain work of fiction for disdain and resolves to get in her good graces by describing the novel as not up to his standards either, unaware that they are discussing a novel she has written. With his discovery of his faux pas, the story is suspended.

Seemingly at a loss for a means to resolve the narrative tension between the insulted Clara James and the increasingly attracted Cameron Frank, the author asks readers to write in with possible endings for the story. This strategy would appear to have been less than successful, as subsequent issues of the magazine lack any mention of the story, its ending, or the fate of its two protagonists. There are, nonetheless, a few features present in the aborted attempt at creative storytelling that would remain constant in the publication's short fiction. The women are generally new to urban environments, self-affirmed, and described in ways aimed at highlighting their intellect and character, as opposed to their sexuality or desire for marriage. The men are respectable and hardworking but harbor character traits that keep them from reaching their full potential. This last is true even within the context of marriage.

Also in the March 1917 issue, a story by another frequent contributor to the fiction pages of *Half-Century Magazine,* Maggie Shaw Fullilove's "Navy Blue Velvet," chronicles the trials of a young African American wife and mother who, despite her husband's objections, spends fifty dollars of her own money to buy a coat made of navy blue velvet.[4] As the story unfolds, the protagonist, Alice, is about to compound her rebellion by attending an upcoming theatrical event wearing the problematic garment, as well as the new hat and shoes she felt obliged to purchase to complement the new dress. Her purchases and intended night out are without her husband's sanction. Indeed, he has no idea any of it is taking place. Once he discovers her in all of her finery, and upon learning of her trip to the theater, he assumes she is seeing another man, and the clothes and evening out serve as proof of the affair. Upon having her deceptions discovered, Alice finds herself in the middle of a battle that threatens her marriage and leads her to contemplate leaving both her husband and her children. He attacks first, screaming:

> "Damn you! . . . You Liar! You wanton liar. . . . You sneaky, low down, huzzy! Going to the theaters with men—cheap, low devilish shows, which nothing but harlots and wenches, like yourself attend! My Children's [sic] mother! Bah! I'll thrash you to the very inch of your life and send you to your daddy. I won't have you—I've done with you forever." (4)

Though her husband may have gotten in the first word, Alice, not to be outdone, quickly collects herself and responds that she deserves to have freedom, access to urban entertainment venues, and pleasure as she sees fit. She believes that because she earned the money she spent to provide herself with these diversions, he should just keep quiet. She yells:

> "Stop! You mean, narrow cur! Your soul is not as big as a puppy's. You self-righteous fool—you don't know what righteousness is! You stingy, whelp—you don't know what beauty and goodness is. . . . Look at me, Mr. Harding. I bought this dress with the first money I ever owned—that fifty dollars you wanted me to place in the bank to buy shoats with—shoats! I hate pigs; and brute husbands are no better than pigs! I am hungry for something beautiful. I've never had anything I wanted—I'm starved. But I shall hunger no longer—I'll go where I please and wear what I please!" (8)

The home's marital discord, while continuing for a number of weeks, is resolved when the husband realizes that even a level-headed woman needs finery and entertainment from time to time and that it is his responsibility to make sure that Alice does not feel the need to sneak around behind his back in order to have that which all women desire and, more importantly, deserve. He makes amends by purchasing a coat for her that she circled in a catalog but had resolved to refrain from buying in order to maintain calm in the household.

Even when married, women in these stories are portrayed as able to earn money, and as desirous of spending it in ways that meet with their own approval. While the story about Clara James does not mention where she has moved from, that she lives in a rooming house suggests she is not from Chicago. Alice's hesitant embrace of fashion and entertainment likewise indicates that such things are new for her. The female protagonists in these stories want to feel good about themselves and are able to identify the behaviors and products that will help them do so. Within all these stories, it is male behavior that is described as problematic and in need of change if relationships are to continue and thrive.

This view of African American women as wives and wage earners was significantly different from that found in magazine fiction aimed at middle-class white women in the early years of the twentieth century. Indeed, in *Ladies' Home Journal* and *Good Housekeeping* (two publications begun late in the nineteenth century and aimed at white middle-class readers), the fiction was ultimately opposed to women's autonomy and ability to earn money of their own. Female protagonists merely spend money their husbands are able to earn and then only on items that would benefit the family. Turn-of-the-century magazines like *Ladies' World*, aimed at poor and rural white women, were full of fictional narratives wherein the protagonists earn money selling clothes they have made and food they have grown to purchase commodities that enhance the living standard of their family, while middle-class protagonists in the fiction of magazines like *Ladies' Home Journal* chose to give up money making to devote their time and energy to the emotional welfare of their families. Wage earning for them was virtually verboten; one would never see a story where the wife would take money she had earned and purchase clothes and an evening of entertainment solely for herself. Nor do such stories portray women like Clara James who live alone and, as near as we can tell, earn their own money and seem uninterested in capturing the romantic attentions of the first available male character. Indeed, that urban space in *Half-Century Magazine* is represented as a key site for male change and female growth and consumption is but one indication and occasion to demonstrate such changes. More than sexual interaction or domestic security, women in the stories desire freedom, choice, and respect. Product consumption is but one path to those ultimate goals, not a destination in and of itself.

By the 1950s, fictional stories in African American women's magazines were replaced in *Tan Confessions* with others of quite a different origin. In this publication, discussions of African American women's sexual desire and consumption practices are focused in entirely new directions.

TAN CONFESSIONS

The cover of the second issue of *Tan Confessions,* in December 1950 (figure 20), is a visual narrative of a significant aspect of the magazine's content, aims, and editorial concerns. The image of a slim, scantily clad African American woman fills three-quarters of the page. She reclines across and substantially covers the prostrate body of an African American man. Her manicured fingers stroke his face; her heavily lipsticked mouth is slightly parted; her eyes gaze longingly down from beneath precisely plucked eyebrows. She leans in as if for a kiss. It is an image of sexual self-assurance and a promise of longing soon to be fulfilled. Though the cover image asks viewers to join what would appear to be an intimate moment, she, focused solely on that which she desires, offers neither a coy smile or the inclusive gaze viewers might have expected. Indeed, the model spares no glance in the direction of her audience. We are witness to an interaction that, though enacted on the public space of a magazine cover, is coded as private. In short, the cover makes clear that *Tan Confessions* believes African American female sexual desire to be a commodity suitable for public consumption. Indeed, such desire can be purchased for the twenty-five-cent cover price.

While the cover image makes explicit the publication's focus on the commodification of sexual desire, *Tan Confessions* also in-

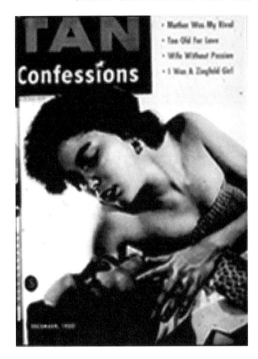

20. *Tan Confessions*
inaugural cover

cluded a Home Magazine and a Special Features section placed
near the end of the publication and in the midst of the sensationalized stories of urban sexual adventure. Those mini-publications
were edited by an African American woman named Frieda de
Knight and included articles and columns devoted, as the editorial
"Letter of Welcome" for the magazine would explain in the
November 1950 first issue, to the most "extensive home-making
coverage in the Negro field with articles on hair, beauty, child
care, health, cooking, interior decoration, party giving, fashions,
and shopping" (1). The articles were interspersed with first-person
accounts in the Special Features section, written by African American women (such as Sarah Vaughn and Lena Horne) who were
celebrities. In these narratives, they told of marriage, life, and
hardship in ways often indistinguishable from the more sensational stories of sexual intrigue that formed the bulk of the
publication. As a result of the inclusion of both the Home Maga-

zine and Special Features section, *Tan Confessions* becomes a publication that first creates, and then struggles mightily to commodify, tensions between didactic instruction about "proper" behavior, attitude, and appearance within the confines of an urban home and marriage, and cultural fantasies about African American female sexual desire outside of that arena. That is, while the magazine would faithfully chronicle the sexual exploits of African American women in its pages and, indeed, profit handsomely from such a focus, it would also go to great lengths to contextualize those exploits within the class-based notions of domesticity that centered around the consumption of products as a marker of both progress and acceptability. Readers were led to believe that while U.S. culture and society at large may have been less than willing to welcome them into nonsegregated public spaces, one means of ensuring their acceptance once these political barriers were removed was to emulate the larger community's interest in product consumption.

There are striking differences between African American migration to urban areas in earlier periods and that during the Second World War. The migration of the 1940s was primarily motivated by economics. After 1942 and the depletion of the white labor supply, the escalation of the war, and the executive order on fair employment, African American migration increased significantly. Despite the realities of poor housing and public health, vice, crime, and discrimination, by the end of the war in 1945, African Americans were optimistic regarding their status in postwar America. After assisting the country at home and abroad in the war effort, they overwhelmingly expected the social, political, and economic rights guaranteed by the Constitution to be theirs. Part of this optimism was attributable to the employment opportunities made possible by the war economy, which in turn facilitated an improved economic condition.[5] As African Americans prepared to launch a civil rights movement against the forces of racism, their marginal relationship to capitalist commercial culture was transformed, as Dwight Brooks has pointed out, in a manner unique "to a people desperately seeking participation in the mainstream of an American society that was becoming increasingly obsessed with consumption as a way of life."[6] In publications aimed at an African American female reading audience, the "consumption obsession" superseded earlier concerns with marriage, manners, morals, and refinement as the most expedient ways to ensure political advancement.

Readers of the first issue of *Tan Confessions* in November 1950 were treated to seven stories of love, romance, and sexual scandal. A teenage girl fights her mother for her boyfriend's affection and sexual attention; a thirty-something spinster discovers the man who helps her find true love and sexual fulfillment (this after subjecting herself to months of unsatisfying sex with her workplace supervisor); and a newly married wife struggles to overcome frigidity and her mother's admonitions in order to find sexual happiness with her new husband. In fulfilling the promise of the image on the cover, all of the stories foreground African American women as sexual beings who are aggressive in addressing their desire for carnal fulfillment. However, these three stories are neatly resolved when the women in question choose to find sexual fulfillment in the context of a marriage that brings them love but also allows them to purchase the products that for them signify status, respectability, and genteel living.[7]

Significantly, in a seeming effort to underline the economic promise and possibility of domestic stability, the first issue of the Home Magazine offered advice on baking "Thanksgiving Treats," as well as suggestions on "Modern Lamps" and more generalized "Home Hints" that point readers toward "This Month's Best Buys in New Products," as well as toward other products designed to "Stop Tooth Decay." Other articles in that section featured the wives of celebrities, describing what married life with their husbands was like. In short, while one portion of the magazine would image African American female sexual desire as problematically present outside the confines of a committed domestic relationship, another would provide advice on harnessing sexual desire in order to properly manage the mechanics of an ongoing domestic relationship and

21. A new reading thrill,
Tan Confessions, 1950

would exemplify and celebrate matrimonial success. Sexual paths, though well traveled month to month, eventually led to domesticity, which equaled sexual fulfillment, which provided African American women economic privilege. Though *Tan Confessions* may not have provided the "thrill" predicted for all its readers in the first advertisement for the new publication (figure 21), it certainly offered a reading experience that was, to say the least, substantially different from anything that had come before. In *Tan Confessions,* women are told that they will have to change if their relationships are to be successful. In opposition to the fluid nature of the stories found in the earlier *Half-Century Magazine,* where an author might dare to ask readers to suggest an interesting ending for her stories, *Tan Confessions* relied upon a consistently recognizable confessional narrative form to sell its magazine during the two years it was in existence, from 1950 to 1952.[8]

CONSUMING FANTASIES IN BLACK AND TAN

John Johnson, the editor, owner, and publisher of *Ebony Magazine,* founded *Tan Confessions* in November 1950, five years to the day after *Ebony Magazine* made its debut. In the premier issue of *Tan Confessions*, he told readers that the magazine would focus on an aspect of African American life that was virtually ignored in the mainstream press, "the happiness, triumphs, sorrows, and suffering of the troubled heart." He went on to explain that "the emotional, intimate experiences of people who never make the headlines are drama in real life that is more graphic, moving and heart-rending than any Hollywood movie" (2). While many readers of the first issue were enthusiastic, writing in to say that *Tan Confessions* was a laudable example of "colored trash" that had been a long time coming, others complained that the magazine's claim of authenticity was laughable, as in a letter in the December 1950 issue: "No respectable colored woman would allow herself to be in these situations and she certainly wouldn't write about them if she did" (5). Though this statement is possibly true, the magazine went to great lengths to ensure that readers believed they were privy to the thoughts, feelings, and sexual desires of real-life African American women, even to the point of posting calls for submissions in both *Ebony* and *Tan Confessions*.[9]

Toward that end, the image accompanying a story in the November 1950 issue that announces that Carolyn has a secret sin pictures an African American woman sitting alone in a chair (figure 22). A separate image rests beside the first. There, an African American man casts a wide and ominous shadow and would appear to be watching our Carolyn as she sits quietly. The caption fills in some of the details as to why she looks so sad and as to who the male figure might be. We are told that she is thinking about the night her "romance was almost wrecked when she had to share the secret of her one sinful night with her future mate." As Carolyn tells readers about this horrendous evening, she is seated at her dressing table and gazing at the photograph of Lonnie, the man who still agreed to marry her despite her having been raped years before. As the story unfolds, we learn that Carolyn, when she was but a teenager too trusting of the boyfriend she thought she loved, allowed herself to be in a deserted hotel room alone with him. Her boyfriend was not able to control

22. "My Secret Sin"

himself, and despite Carolyn's pleas to stop, he raped her. Lonnie, after a moment of anger because his lovely Carolyn was mistreated, holds her in his arms and tells her he loves her and always will. He also cautions her against allowing her fear to keep her from sharing her thoughts with him in the future. He tells her that secrets, shame, and fear are the only things that will ever drive him away (23, 77–81). While in an earlier period, the secret a wife kept from her husband would be constructed as an opportunity for him to change his behavior and assumptions about who his wife is and what women needed, in the pages of *Tan Confessions*, African American women would consistently be instructed to change themselves and their behavior, as well as to reorder their internal lives, if they wished to have and keep a husband.

In *Tan Confessions,* urban desire for sexual fulfillment was communicated in a first-person confessional narrative style long a staple of women's writing in magazine fiction. Indeed the genre's roots date back to 1919 and a magazine entitled *True Story.*[10] That magazine was followed decades later by *True Confessions,* which would serve as both namesake and inspiration for John Johnson's 1950 enterprise. While *True Confessions* would claim a white working-class audience, *Tan Confessions* offered elite African American women as protagonists. That difference means the latter publication differed in significant ways from the one upon which it was reportedly based. However, in regard to the use of confessional discourse, they are mirror images. Within the confessional format, privileged African American women wrapped in the arms of their new husbands tell of having to sell their babies when they were young and trapped in unplanned pregnancies (figure 23), talk about their horror at having male

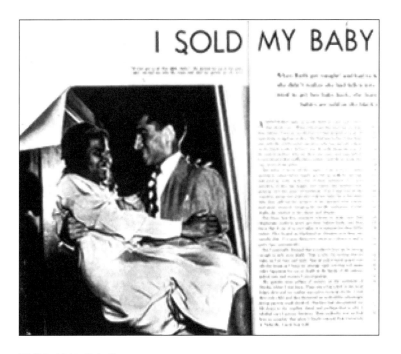

23. "I Sold My Baby"

teachers make sexual demands, as well as force them to take drugs in exchange for passing grades, and describe their shame and repentance for their sexual affairs outside the confines of their marriages. Roseanne Mandziuk has pointed out that confessional discourses at the turn of the twentieth century tended to perform three functions for their women readers: "First the stories functioned as therapeutic messages promising benefits and rewards to women. Second, they provided didactic instruction on proper behavior and modern ways. Third, the commodity confessionals served as interrogative texts that raised questions abut cultural proscriptions for women."[11]

Mandziuk argues that the confessional format allowed working-class readers to identify with the narrator's struggle to rise above her difficulties and to rid herself of the shame of material deprivation in a society that judged her harshly as a result. While probably true in relation to white working-class women, the source of shame for the middle-class African American protagonists and readers of *Tan Confessions* is not spelled out but would seem to connect to the possibility of the characters coming close to losing the economic privilege and lifestyles they have always known. For example, in the November 1950 story about Carolyn's sinful secret, we are told that she came from a wealthy, two-parent background and almost lost the advantages that it should have ensured on that fateful night when her rough and uncouth boyfriend raped her (77). This message is underscored when Carolyn tells readers that in addition to her husband's love, she almost lost the class advantages she had accrued as a result of having married well.

The possibility of unchecked and inappropriate sexual desire's leading to the loss of economic privilege is explored in another story in the same issue of *Tan Confessions*. In "Strange Love," Yvonne, the wife of a young lawyer who works long hours to provide for her, finds herself in the midst of a burgeoning lesbian relationship with Willa. The caption for the story tells readers: "An exotic woman stole this wife from her husband. But true love finally won out over the tainted affair" (16). Readers learn that

24. Willa and Yvonne's "Strange Love"

the two women met in an intimate little art gallery and bonded over numerous shopping trips. Willa is an "exotic beauty" who was not shy about paying compliments and providing companionship for the very lonely Yvonne, who has money but no friends, while Willa is an independent woman of independent economic means. Yvonne becomes less interested in their friendship once she discovers that Willa is interested only in a sexual relationship and has no desire to allow her to be a stay-at-home wife with time for shopping and leisurely trips to art galleries. All ends happily when Yvonne chooses to return to the husband, who, she tells readers, loves her and decides to forgive her on the condition that she promise not to give herself over to her "wild side" again.

As a group, the stories in *Tan Confessions* portray middle-class African American women who choose to turn their backs on pasts and presents marked by sexual experiences outside of marriage. It is the threat of losing their marital status that provides the bulk of the narrative tension. Perhaps the uneasy fit engendered in the process of transforming the confessional genre from one that addressed the material longing of working-class white women to one that emphasized the hard-won significance of marriage as a sure route to class privilege might account for the short tenure of the publication. Yet the inclusion of well-off African American women who were imaged as active consumers functioned as a beginning for the inclusion of African American women in the culture of consumption so much a part of post–World War II U.S. society. *Tan Confessions* relied upon an ideological construct that suggested to African American women that one means of both conforming to accepted gender norms and combating race-based discrimination was to consume.

Within white American culture, similar calls for consumption were linked with post–World War II formulations of patriotism and citizenship and were deployed to help ameliorate Cold War and Atomic Age paranoia. While African Americans were substantially absent from such discussions and representations in the dominant culture, this was far from the case in *Tan Confessions*. At the same time it constructed African American female desire as a saleable commodity, the magazine offered images and representations of African American women as a ready and willing consumer market. The two narratives were connected: Though sexual desire could be present outside of the bounds of marriage and domesticity, product consumption could not.

Given that the Home Magazine and Special Features sections would bear the brunt of the responsibility for communicating *Tan Confessions*'s message of consumption and its relationship to marriage and stable notions of domesticity, and that the magazine shared such a crucial relationship to the images of women and consumption in *Ebony,* an explication of the relationship of African American women to consumption as imagined in *Ebony* will prove instructive. Indeed, one of John Johnson's major accomplishments with *Ebony* was finding a method, rationale, and rhetoric for selling major manufacturers on the possibility of making more money from an untapped African American consumer market. Yet in that publication, the relationship of African American women to consumption was never fully outlined.

While very little work has focused either on an African American culture of consumption in general, or on the specific relationship of African American women's identity to that construct in either white or African American magazines, to do either topic justice, *Ebony* must take center stage.[12] A look at issues of *Ebony* from 1945 through 1955 reveals that the fiction in *Tan Confessions*, as well as the Home Magazine and Special Features sections of the publication, were part of a larger strategy to construct and market particular forms of African American female identity to African Americans and to white advertisers and manufacturers. That is, African Americans were taught about particular types of acceptable identity right along with the advertising executives who provided the financing necessary to keep Johnson's publishing empire afloat.

EBONY DREAMS: BUYING CITIZENSHIP, SELLING RACE

John Johnson started *Ebony Magazine* in November 1945 with very little national advertising; accordingly, the prognosis for its success was not encouraging. In keeping with the assessments of many of how to build a firm economic base for African Americans, and drawing on tried and true representational strategies from the nineteenth century, Johnson chose to accentuate the positive and prosperous in African American life. His proclamation that the magazine would "not harp on the race question" served a twofold purpose in the successful growth of the magazine (2). It provided prosperous African Americans a place to showcase their successes and offered inspirational blueprints for others as they attempted to reach similar heights. For national advertisers, such a focus gestured toward the possibility of a largely untapped source of revenue from the African American community. A magazine that catered to and portrayed the exceptional personalities, opinion leaders, and their followers in African American life provided a suitable nonthreatening medium in which advertisers could promote their products and further enhance industry profits.

A November 1955 article entitled "*Ebony* Pioneers in Negro Advertising: Magazine Leads Merchants to $16 Billion Negro

Market" outlined Johnson's strategy in relation to the advertising industry, his magazine, and the "un-tapped" African American consumer market: "When *Ebony*'s first 25,000 copies appeared on the nation's newsstands in 1945 as a brand-new magazine, born full grown, but lacking the familiar pages of all-important advertising, some skeptics took one look, and sympathetically prophesied that it was destined for inevitable doom. For they knew that without the sustaining advertising of America's giants of industry, no such magazine could hope to attain success" (8).

While numerous African American newspapers existed during the 1950s, their circulation was racially and regionally limited. They were, in addition, often viewed as little more than organs of protest against racial discrimination in local governmental and business concerns.[13] Convincing white manufacturers and advertisers that there was a layer of African American society willing and financially able to purchase their products, and that such a group was influenced by what they read in the African American press, was *Ebony*'s most difficult selling job. Through the years, the personality spreads, success stories, and other celebratory articles in *Ebony*, along with its increases in circulation and readership, served to suggest to advertisers that their share of this sizeable untapped market could be maximized if they specifically targeted it. Most manufacturers then thought of African Americans as a homogenous group with little or no disposable income. Johnson's magazine attempted to change such perceptions by portraying only an African American elite. This strategy, Johnson believed, would lead to racial and economic advancement for African Americans as a group. In a November 1955 editorial, we see the strategy boldly stated: "Few, if any, of America's major advertisers believed there was any need for inviting Negroes to buy the best food, the 'label' brands of clothing, the better cars, or even the popular brands of toothpaste and fingernail polish. . . . Today, largely because of *Ebony*'s stories which picture the Negro as a person who works, who is professional, who is respectable— merchants who sell the finest products are convinced that Negroes are worth seeking out" (7).

Before he could cash in on his idea, Johnson first had to prove that there was a group of African Americans who had the values in place to become viable consumers and desirable citizens. Accordingly, the Personality section of the magazine in November 1955 included articles about such diverse subjects as a woman in Dallas who gave away $325,000 dollars in property to charity, an interview with the world's oldest working man (he was 113), and a young girl who had just won a nationally televised spelling bee and planned to use her winnings to attend college.[14] Because Johnson believed that in order to sell African Americans to major manufacturers he first had to correct stereotypical beliefs, his magazine made sure to point out that African Americans were, for example, not lazy. On the contrary, the Personality section would seem to say, they work until they are 113 years old; they are not dumb, because an African American just won a nationally televised spelling bee; they are not all poor, because here is a woman who just gave away a large sum of money. With those derogatory notions out of the way, Johnson could focus on the similarities between African American and white middle-class consumers. Given the success of *Ebony*, which amassed $10 million in advertising revenue within its first three years, it is clear that Johnson's strategy was not only on target but also profitable.[15]

A close look at the content of other sections of *Ebony* evidences comparable narratives. The entertainment column in the November 1950 issue included such wide-ranging features as candid photographs of famous white entertainers snapped by Sammy Davis Jr., articles on African Americans who have or want to have minor roles in new movies, and a story about a young nightclub singer who includes a donkey in her act—in spite of the obstacles the animal may present for her, she has persevered (22, 47, 56). Such stories fairly shout that African Americans are able to overcome adversity, desire any type of employment offered, and can be comfortable in the presence of and accepted by whites. Similarly, the section on occupations participated in the effort by proclaiming that thirty-one African American reporters worked for white newspapers, or explaining how the South could not possibly get along without its African American teachers.

The various articles reveal the ways in which race is handled in *Ebony*. Although by 1955 the civil rights movement had begun (the landmark *Brown v. Board of Education* ruling took place in 1954 and the Montgomery bus boycott was in full swing), *Ebony* makes no mention of tension between the races, or of the civil rights movement at all. Race, and by extension racism, was an issue in the magazine only so we can be told of the narrowing difference between the races, or shown how African Americans had absorbed U.S. consumer culture sufficiently to be viewed as nonthreatening "good consumers" and ideal U.S. citizens.

While *Ebony* does much to advance the image of African American women as capable of being and becoming celebrities and model citizens, interestingly, there are few images in *Ebony* of, or narrative content about, married African American women. The majority of women in the advertisements and articles are described as celebrities, actresses, performers, glamour girls, or career women who have achieved some type of first. The magazine has little or nothing to say about African American women within a domestic space, and even less to offer in the way of such women having an internal life or sexual desire. In the pages of *Tan Confessions*, however, considerable attention is paid to the contours of an African American female identity within the context of consumption and its relationship to marriage. *Tan Confessions* builds upon and makes specific assertions about the relationship between marriage, economic privilege, and consumption. That is, marriage and the role of the stay-at-home wife are the subjects of varied discussion and representation, and *Tan Confessions* engages the topic of marriage in a manner that joins narratives about marriage with those about consumption. Such a coupling appears to have been the primary focus of the Home Magazine, along with the Special Features section of *Tan Confessions*.

MARKETING MATRIMONY, SELLING CONSUMPTION

Each issue of *Tan Confessions* began, not with one of the "confessions" about marital infidelity or exploration, but rather with a special feature entitled "How He Proposed." In this monthly column, African American celebrities recounted the moments when their present husbands proposed to them. In a tone and structure similar to that found in the more sensationalized stories, performers like Sarah Vaughn (figure 25) describe the moments when they first met their future husbands and how they became engaged and married. In the November 1950 issue, Vaughn, for example, reports that she met her husband while touring, and after the two of them had been dating for some time, she asked him if he would like to manage her career. He looked at her with a bit of surprise before replying, "Sure, Sass, I'll manage you, but it would be even better if we managed each other" (5). The next day, Vaughn tells us, they went to get a marriage license. In the same issue appears a scandalous "true story" in which the headline describes the storyteller as "Any Man's Woman" and tells readers that she "begged, borrowed, and even stole the affections of any man until she found the love of one man . . . and then almost lost it" (28). This is immediately followed by another special feature column entitled "If You Married . . . Jimmy Edwards." While the husbands one could imagine marrying changed from month to month and included celebrities like Sidney Poitier, this story describes what it was like for Mrs. Edwards to be married to "a handsome, young, down to earth movie star who used to be a CIO organizer" (30). Once again, we hear that married life is wonderful and that the speaker is grateful to have found such a loving supportive spouse. In the final piece in the section, "My Prince Charming," June Eckstein (bandleader Billy Eckstein's wife) "personally tells in her own words" what it was like to have been wooed and won over by her husband. As in the other regular columns, the "Prince Charming" in question changes from month to month but is always a recognizable and well-known star.

Consistently, the Special Features columns portray African American women who are happily married, and it is that status that legitimates their inclusion in the publication. They are either celebrities themselves, or married to well-known performers. Each narrative is written in first person, and all mention some

Popular singer Sarah Vaughan runs through a vocal routine at a night-club rehearsal while her husband and manager, George Treadwell, coaches her.

BY SARAH VAUGHAN

25. Sarah Vaughn, "How He Proposed"

hardship their relationship had to endure before they found love with their husband. In the case of Sarah Vaughn, the hardship was that her husband, trumpet player George Treadwell, took so long to ask her to get married that she contemplated embarrassing herself and asking him first, as well as that he had to give up his career as a musician to manage her career. For pianist Hazel Scott, the issue was a bit more complicated, as her minister husband was still married to his first wife at the time that he proposed and they had to wait a year before his divorce was final, the December 1950 issue reported (5). As in the stories written by anonymous contributors, marriage and domesticity are consistently celebrated. Significantly, discussion and representations of marriage are generally tied to images of those who are economically privileged; as a result, the magazine mainly appears to portray such types of African Americans because they are the most interesting and significant members of African American communities. Theirs is an example to be both imitated and celebrated.

While I am in no way trying to suggest that marriage should not be celebrated, I do believe that the discursive function of marriage as represented in *Tan Confessions* does a particular kind of cultural work that connects with the larger aims and concerns of the publication's publisher and founder in relation to positioning African Americans within the culture of consumption. Even when those discussed in relation to marriage are not wealthy or well known, the publication makes a point of highlighting behaviors and characteristics intimately tied to an overarching concern with visualizing and displaying married African American women as they relate to consumption and privilege.

For example, the Home Magazine in each issue of *Tan Confessions* included a column entitled "Dearly Beloved." There, a woman named Frances Abigail Johnson provided marital advice for readers who chose to write to her. In the December 1950 inaugural issue of the column Johnson opined, "The trouble with most marriages . . . is that most people bring more nonsense than common sense to a marriage." Things would run much more smoothly "if both husband and wife would work just as hard at being happily married as business partners work at making their business a success." And finally, "marriage is a partnership and its product (a happy home and family) is more valuable than anything on the market today" (10). Her linking of the rhetoric of business and product consumption to the realm of marriage is underscored in the responses she gives readers to their questions.

Letters in this section were received from readers all over the country, and marital issues ranged from frustration over husbands who would not let wives drive the cars they helped to purchase, to concerns over the levels of drinking, violence, and gambling some women found an unwelcome part of their marriage. Mrs. Rose L., tired of her life as a stay-at-home mother, wrote in to ask what she should do about a husband who is not supportive of her desire to work, and the pressure her young children, five and six years old, are putting on her to stay at home. She complains that her husband is not at all happy about her decision to take a job, because "he says he makes enough to take care of his family and there is no necessity of my working." Rose ends her letter by saying that this is true, and "he takes care of me very well but still I want to get out and work and meet people." In answer to the young mother's request for advice, Jackson suggests that this is a problem she can solve for herself and that all will be well: "*If* your children are happy with a working mother, *if* your husband agrees that it is all right for you to work, and *if* you cannot really be happy without working even though your husband is a good provider, then by all means keep your job" (10; emphasis in original). Given that Rose has written in because her desire to work is causing problems in her marriage, Jackson's response is little more than a dismissal of such concerns. Her allegiance is to a different ideal than that to which Rose is attempting to appeal. If Rose can be well provided for by her husband, there is no reason to entertain her desires for personal fulfillment.

During earlier periods, stories and articles written about women who were attempting to negotiate domestic relationships in urban areas suggested that personal fulfillment and marital commitment could coexist. By the 1950s, due to a conscious process that sought to link ideas of marriage with those encompassing and defining economic privilege, such focuses were no longer as desirable and would not again come to the fore until the mid-1970s, when *Essence Magazine* began publication.

Though stories that featured African American women as urban protagonists were a staple of *Half-Century Magazine* three decades before *Tan Confessions* was first published, the stories, fantasies, and cultural projects that make up *Tan Confessions* are, nonetheless, notable. While the urban tales in *Half-Century Magazine* most often focused on men and their need to make changes if they were to be worthy of the women who wished to be part of their lives, *Tan Confessions* inverted this paradigm. Where the narratives of the earlier publication detailed how men had to grow and change if they were to do justice to the possibilities inherent in the new urban spaces they inhabited, as well as to the women with whom they shared their lives, by the 1950s, the stories featuring African American women in *Tan Confessions* portrayed women as most in need of change if they were desirous of getting and keeping a husband.

Because *Tan Confessions* claimed narrative authenticity, that is, it led readers to believe its stories were written by anonymous African American women and were based on their real-life experiences, it was a significant departure from earlier publications. While in preceding eras, sex and sexual desire were forbidden topics, here, in an effort to both define and shape a market and outlet for African American women's sexual desire and thereby turn desire into a commodity, previously taboo topics are necessarily highlighted. As a result, *Tan Confessions* might easily be described as the final step in the making of modern African American women's magazine culture. It summarizes and contextualizes all of the cultural narratives found in African American women's magazines that had come before it (fashion as respectability, shifting definitions of home in relation to modernity, domesticity as a significant goal, consumption as a progressive means of obtaining citizenship) and, at the same time, functions as a harbinger of many of the film and television narratives and representations of African American womanhood that would come after.

7

But Is It Black and Female?

Essence, O, and American Magazine Publishing

There are a lot of unanswered questions marketers still have about our audience. *Essence* is the gateway to that audience.

—*Michelle Eubanks, Essence Group Publisher*

In my 15 years of dealing with people and their dysfunctions, day in and day out, I've learned that the word that most defines this decade, even this century, is disconnect. What this magazine does is reconnect people to what deserves priority and to bring meaning to their lives.

—*Oprah Winfrey*

WHEN I began this project, I believed it would primarily focus on *Essence Magazine* and the African American women's magazines that came after it. After beginning what I believed to be "background research" on the magazines that preceded *Essence,* I came to understand that the cultural issues, narrative strategies, and economic significance of that publication were best understood within the historical context of those earlier publications. But this project would be incomplete without some mention of *Essence.* It was a significant undertaking and has continued to be an important influence for the thirty-plus years since its founding in May 1970. While I dispute the truth of the general belief that it is the first popular magazine for African American women, it has certainly lasted for far longer than any of the previously discussed publications and is much more widely known than any of the African American women's magazines that came before it.

Today, its significance lies less in its editorial policies, fashion pages, or political content than in its success as a gateway through which mainstream advertisers are able to reach a lucrative group of African American consumers of both genders. In that sense, it is a profitable example of U.S. magazine-publishing industry practices. The magazine's founders were able to succeed at and modernize a marketing strategy first attempted by John Johnson in the 1950s. Indeed, a *Publishers Weekly* story on March 5, 2001, titled "African Americans Spent $356 Million on Books in 2000," credits *Essence* with an ability to reach upwards of 72 percent of African American book buyers (156). Five African American men founded the magazine. The two founders still living recently decided to sell 49 percent of the publication to Time Warner Communications. This led me to wonder if it was still accurate to refer to it as an African American women's magazine. Certainly it is and has always been edited by African American women, and just as surely, its imagined readership is overwhelmingly African American and female (one-third of the contemporary readership is male). However, I was less than sure that, given the gender of the publication's founders and its recent sale to a white corporation, it would at present fit within the parameters of the study I outlined when I first decided I wanted to write a cultural history of African American women's magazines owned, edited by, and aimed at African American women.

In an even more difficult moment of categorization, I began to think about *O, the Oprah Magazine*. Started in 2000, this publication has transformed magazine publishing and is an unqualified success. Winfrey and her business partner in the venture, Hearst Publishing, with little advance marketing, were able to sell out the initial newsstand run of 1.6 million copies. In a few short months the publication signed up 1.9 million subscribers (by way of comparison, American *Vogue* has 1.1 million). Featuring an image of

Winfrey, an African American woman, on the cover of each issue, the magazine outsells more established rivals like *In Style, Glamour, Harper's Bazaar*, and *Good Housekeeping*. In addition to appearing on the cover, Winfrey approves the layout and advertising for each issue and provides content via a monthly interview with inspirational figures, as well as a column called "What I Know for Sure," in which she offers her feelings on various personal-growth issues. However, far more than defining her audience as African American, her success is testament to her ability to rely on a kind of universality that crosses age, race, and class lines and appeals to professional women of all ethnicities. While clearly *O* is a women's magazine owned by an African American woman, I was not quite sure it was an African American women's magazine. Such women are not precluded from purchasing and reading the magazine, but neither is it marketed specifically to them.

While these two contemporary magazines obviously demand more nuanced definitions of race, gender, and ownership than did those African American women's publications that came before, they also tell us quite a bit about a post–civil rights, post–Black power, post-integration use, meaning, and significance of both race and gender in the United States, as well as about African American magazine culture. They tell us that in many ways times have changed; they are a testament to the success of the political movements and struggles of past generations. They make clear that in some areas, such movements have paid tangible dividends. In relation to questions about ownership, marketing strategy, and an ability to locate African Americans firmly within a culture of consumption, they are at the same time substantially dependent on what came before, and a world apart.

ESSENCE MAGAZINE

The idea for what would become a magazine for African American women began in a seminar attended largely by African American men. One of these men, Earl Lewis, was then a banker who wanted to take his life in a different direction. When offered the opportunity, he jumped at the chance to attend the seminar, which was geared toward aspiring African American entrepreneurs. Though he knew nothing about publishing, when someone mentioned that a magazine for African American women might be a good idea, he got started on the venture that would become *Essence Magazine*.[1] Lewis, Jonathan Blount, Cecil Hollingsworth, and Clarence O. Smith, all African American men who attended the same session on entrepreneurship, formed a business concern named the Hollingsworth Group, and then created a magazine that promised African American women that it would "speak in your name and in your voice." After making sure readers knew the publishers intended to present information "from a Black perspective—that will necessarily include the full spectrum of Black women," the publishers' statement ends by saying its aim will be to "delight and to celebrate the beauty, pride, strength, and uniqueness of all Black Women."[2]

26. *Essence Magazine* publishing group

Today Lewis is still the publisher, and Smith is the president. The other two men pictured in the photographs accompanying the publisher's statement (figure 26), Jonathan Blount and Cecil Hollingsworth, left the company within the first few years because of differing views over its direction, as had a fifth member in 1969, a year before the magazine was published. While the nature of the conflict over the magazine's focus is less than clear, the first issue of the magazine would, as promised by the publishers, be a heady mix of Black nationalist ideologies, public affairs, fashion, and homemaking advice. Though the particulars of its business strategy would change over the years, it would ultimately find the perfect mix of fashion, politics, and racial meanings to interest both African American female readers and white business concerns. It crafted a narrative of African American womanhood that was popular, relevant, and lucrative.

The letters to the editor written in response to the first issue echo the responses to the African American women's magazines that came before it. Some thank the publishers for making it possible for them to stop reading magazines that "didn't have me in mind" when they were published; others promised to be longtime readers and congratulated the publication on its success.[3] The magazine positioned African American female readers within a 1970s Black nationalist rhetoric and discourse that drew upon varying aspects of their identity. They rejected feminism. They were warriors, at the forefront of political struggles for racial advancement. They were strong women who stood by their men. They were queens unable to understand why their kings slept with and married white women. They were women who were Black, and race mattered greatly to them. They did not wish to embrace dominant constructions of femininity.

Very much influenced by and engaged with the cultural and political movements that called for Black power, the first issue featured an article entitled "Revolt: From Rosa to Kathleen" about African American women's involvement with militant groups, causes, and organizations, beginning with Rosa Parks and ending with Black Panther Party member Kathleen Cleaver. The

27. *Essence* inaugural issue

renowned associate professor of psychiatry at Harvard University
Dr. Alvin Poussaint suggested in his column that African American
women were victims "of a special form of oppression." He went
on to explain: "For instance, most Blacks are angry. Are Black
women even more angry because of their double oppression? Are
they more resentful and jealous of male status than are white

women? Do they feel more competitive toward Black males than white males, or vice versa? Are Black women more docile or do they show more compensatory toughness and aggression? Does their situation make them more or less interested in sex?" Poussaint ends by telling readers that there are no easy answers to such questions and that we need to study how our African heritage has influenced these patterns. In what seemed to be almost an answer to Poussaint's question about African American women's interest in sex, the cover article of the inaugural issue asked, "Sensual Black Man, Do You Love Me?" Fiction writer Louise Meriwether wrote about African American men's sexual preferences for white women and lack of interest in those who were African American. These subjects were interspersed with fashion pages that focused on hair—"Dynamite Afros"—and clothes (see figure 28).

What the magazine did not have was much advertising. Indeed, while the first issue had thirteen pages of advertising, the next two would have only five (today, a profitable magazine aims for between 52 and 55 percent ads). By far the largest hurdle faced by the magazine's founders was convincing advertisers that African American women were viable consumers. Perhaps this concern with advertising and the need for a more marketable image of African Americans capable of enticing mainstream companies to support the magazine explains the fact that *Essence* would, by the end of the third year, drastically reduce its focus on Black power and Black nationalism in the lives of everyday African Americans, increase the number of articles that focused on celebrities, and put a much heavier focus on fashion and beauty. No longer would African American women be placed firmly in the midst of a radical political narrative. No, by the middle of the 1970s, they would be shown to have a far greater interest in clothes, travel, and cosmetics than in political struggle.

According to Lewis, it took six years for the magazine to break even and much longer for advertisers' perceptions to change. And it has just been since 1996 that "the magazine has attracted many premium-priced brands, particularly in the health- and beauty-aids market, that had once eschewed the market and are now

28. *Essence* fashion page, 1970

aggressively advertising" in it.[4] Early in the 1980s, *Essence*'s management team began to expand into other ventures. In 1984 it
launched an Essence-by-Mail mail-order catalog that features
fashions, soft goods, and art objects. That same year, it began syn-
dication of a television half-hour show, which ran for four years.
Essence Television Productions, Inc., now produces a prime-time

network special, the Essence Awards, which honor achievements of African Americans. A licensing division launched in 1984 sells the Essence name to a collection of sewing patterns from the Butterick Company, as well as to lines of eyeglasses and hosiery. In an effort to apply its strategy beyond African American women, in 1998, Essence Communications founded, provided the capital for, and took a majority share of *Latina Magazine*.[5]

Much more than a mere association with African American women, the magazine and name now stand for successful business and marketing practices and are a testament to the efficacy of a business strategy that was first enacted by John Johnson twenty-five years before *Essence* was founded. It first constructs a particular meaning of African American femaleness and then connects that meaning to a discourse of consumption; the whole is then delivered to major marketing concerns. While in earlier periods, it would have been unimaginable for a publication aimed at, and filled with images of, African American women to entice such business interest, by the 1980s, these women were income producing and highly visible. The interest in and comfort with images of African Americans would not be disconnected from the decade's later success of *O*. Part of the success of *Essence* was its focus on the particularities of race and gender in such a manner as to construct a consumer group. Oprah Winfrey's success would lie in her ability to disconnect particularized and narrow racial meanings about her body from an interest in the product she wanted to sell. Indeed, her body has become one of the biggest marketing devices available to the publication.

O, THE OPRAH MAGAZINE

In the contemporary culture of U.S. publishing, most believe that celebrity sells. Given the presumed truth of this adage, it is tempting to assume that the success of the magazine that bears Winfrey's name is a result of her celebrity status. While perhaps partly true, to focus merely on celebrity would be to overlook the significance of the magazine. Unlike the other publications discussed in this book, *O* has a broad readership and appeal that cuts across

29. *O, the Oprah Magazine,* 2003

lines of race and class. Also unique is the fact that, as a result of the success of publications when she appeared on their covers, Winfrey was approached by a group of businesspeople who thought she would be able to make a success of a magazine published by her. She did not conceive of the idea herself. In a life and career that is full of firsts, that she is the first African American woman to universalize meanings of race in a popular context is but one of many. An African American woman owns the publication. She appears on each of its covers. She has significant say in its editorial and advertising content. However, it is not an African American women's magazine. Perhaps that is the most notable first of all.

O is a magazine that positions itself as for and about professional women who have an interest in spirituality and are attempting to negotiate the day-to-day realities of their lives. Its readership draws heavily upon, but is not solely composed of, women who watch her television show.[6] However, it does bear striking similarities to her show's mix of advice, spirituality, beauty, fashion, health, lifestyle, and fitness. While meaningful in the lives of its readers on a personal level, it is also a successful business enterprise based on a winning strategy that has alerted marketers that "spirituality has come alive in the marketplace." Those who work for the magazine add that, because its readership is more affluent than those who watch daytime television and read many other women's magazines, the publication "opens up new market opportunities."[7] For example, when Winfrey appeared on one cover wearing an expensive evening gown, the manufacturer reportedly was swamped with orders for the gown from women of all sizes all over the country.

A recent issue of the publication gave advice on balancing one's life and help with feeling centered. Another article offered advice for women who believed themselves to be workaholics, while a third suggested it might be time for an emotional checkup and asks, "How are you—*really*?" Though in many ways substantially similar to other publications aimed at women in general, it is primarily driven by the issues and concerns of its founder and an understanding of contemporary womanhood that privileges self-care and emotional support. Unlike the women who founded and owned African American women's magazines in earlier periods, like *Ringwood's Journal* and *Half-Century Magazine,* in this publication, Winfrey need not attempt to fit herself or other African American women into constructs and ideologies designed for white American women. Quite simply, she is able to redefine femininity and womanhood so that its meaning assumes the inclusion of African Americans. Perhaps the most significant aspect of the publication is that it makes questions about its blackness irrelevant. I still wonder, though: Is it an African American women's magazine?

Notes

ONE. SCATTERED PAGES

1. Noliwe Rooks, *Hair Raising: Beauty, Culture, and African American Women* (New Brunswick: Rutgers University Press, 1996).
2. Walter Daniel, *Black Journals of the United States* (Westport, Conn.: Greenwood Press, 1982), 194.
3. Frankie Hutton, *The Early Black Press in America, 1827–1860* (Westport, Conn.: Greenwood Press, 1992), 57–59, argues that women have been unfairly described as oppressed by patriarchal sentiments in African American newspapers and by male editors. In terms of the historical context of women in the African American press, Hutton points out that during slavery, it was the activities and sentiments of free women that reached print. What was profiled were the ways in which such women dealt with issues like temperance, education, and general methods for uplifting the race, as well as articles that countered negative images of African American women. This was accomplished through reporting the females' good deeds and community service.
4. Bill Gaskins, artist and professor of photography, Parson's School of Design, in conversation with the author.
5. Ros Ballaster, Margaret Beetham, Elizabeth Frazer, and Sandra Hebron, *Women's Worlds: Ideology, Femininity, and the Woman's Magazine* (London: Macmillan, 1991), 1.
6. Abby Arthur Johnson and Ronald Maberry, *Propaganda and Aesthetics: The Literary Politics of Afro-American Magazines in the Twentieth Century* (Amherst: University of Massachusetts Press, 1979), 10. This work is one of the few to focus solely on magazines in African American culture between 1900 and 1976. While it does not mention any of the magazines discussed here, it does discuss African American magazines in the context of a struggle over propaganda and aesthetics.
7. Ibid., 204.
8. Penelope L. Bullock, *The Afro-American Periodical Press, 1838–1909* (Baton Rouge: Louisiana State University Press, 1981), 210–212.
9. Daniel, *Black Journals*, 130, 373.

10. Ibid.,150.
11. *The Crisis*, November 1910, 2.
12. Ibid.
13. Deborah Gray White, *Too Heavy a Load: Black Women in Defense of Themselves, 1884–1994* (New York: W. W. Norton, 1999), 71.
14. Saartje Baartman (the "Hottentot Venus") and the spectacle of her naked body when exhibited in London is a prime example of this phenomenon. She tried to don Western dress to downplay her difference from European society. The most thorough account of her life and death is a film by Zola Maseko, *The Life and Times of Sara Baartman, "The Hottentot Venus"* (New York: First Run Films, 1999).
15. Deborah Gray White, *Ar'n't I a Woman? Female Slaves in the Plantation South* (New York: W. W. Norton, 1985), 29–33.
16. Paula Giddings, *When and Where I Enter: The Impact of Black Women on Race and Sex in America* (New York: William Morrow, 1984), 35.
17. Lucinda H. MacKethan, "Metaphors of Mastery in the Slave Narratives," in *The Art of Slave Narrative: Original Essays in Criticism and Theory*, ed. John Sekora and Darwin Turner (Macomb: Western Illinois University Press, 1982), 55.
18. "Black Letters; Or Uncle Tom-Foolery in Literature," *Graham's Magazine* (February 1853): 209.
19. J. Noel Heermance, *William Wells Brown and Clotelle* (North Haven, Conn.: Archon Books, 1969), 26–27.
20. Marva J. Furman, "The Slave Narrative: Prototype of the Early Afro-American Novel," in *The Art of Slave Narrative: Original Essays in Criticism and Theory*, ed. John Sekora and Darwin Turner (Macomb: Western Illinois University, 1982), 26–27.
21. Ibid., 28.
22. *Running a Thousand Miles to Freedom; or, The Escape of William and Ellen Craft from Slavery* (1860), in *Great Slave Narratives*, ed. Arna Bontemps (Boston: Beacon Press, 1969), 274–275.
23. It is also interesting to note that while Craft's autobiography is entitled *The Escape of William and Ellen Craft from Slavery*, William's is the only voice we hear. For a fuller discussion of the politics of gender within the slave narrative tradition, see Frances Smith Foster, "'In Respect to Females . . .': Differences in the Portrayals of Women by Male and Female Narrators," *Black American Literature Forum* 15, 2 (summer 1981): 66–70; and Hazel Carby, *Reconstructing Womanhood: The Emergence of the Afro-American Woman Novelist* (New York: Oxford University Press, 1987).
24. *Narrative of the Life and Adventures of Henry Bibb, an American Slave* (1849), in *Puttin' On Ole Massa*, ed. Gilbert Osofsky (New York: Harper and Row, 1969), 169.

25. John Blassingame, *Slave Testimony* (Baton Rouge: Louisiana State University Press, 1977), 376.

26. Jacqueline Jones, *Labor of Love, Labor of Sorrow: Black Women and Work and the Family, from Slavery to the Present* (New York: Vintage Books, 1985), 156–157.

27. Ibid.

28. Deborah Willis, *James Van der Zee, Photographer, 1886–1983* (New York: Harry N. Abrams, 1992), 12.

29. Ibid., 10.

30. Daphne Brooks, "Corpses and (Re)cover(ed) Girls: Lynching, Photography, and Black Feminist Fiction in the NAACP's *Crisis*." Photocopy.

31. Henry Louis Gates, "The Trope of the New Negro and the Reconstruction of the Image of the Black," *Representations* 12 (fall 1988): 124, 135.

32. Lizabeth Cohen, *Making a New Deal: Industrial Workers in Chicago, 1919–1939* (Cambridge: Cambridge University Press, 1990), 189.

33. Ellen Gruber Garvey, *The Adman in the Parlor: Magazines and the Gendering of Consumer Culture, 1880s–1910s* (New York: Oxford University Press, 1996), 18.

34. Richard Ohmann, "Where Did Mass Culture Come From: The Case of the Magazines," in *Politics of Letters* (Middletown, Conn.: Wesleyan University Press, 1987), 28.

35. Martha Banta, *Imaging American Women: Idea and Ideals in Cultural History* (New York: Columbia University Press, 1987), 69. I want to thank Daphne Brooks for sharing her unpublished paper on the *Crisis* magazine cover girls with me and, as a result, leading me to this discussion of types of American women used in advertising during the period.

36. Virginia Wolcott, " 'Bible, Bath and Broom': Nannie Helen Burroughs's National Training School and African American Racial Uplift," *Journal of Women's History* (spring 1997): 88–110.

Two. Refashioning Rape

1. Melton McLaurin, *Celia, a Slave: A True Story* (New York: Avon Books, 1991).

2. *Running a Thousand Miles to Freedom*, 274–275. See also *Narrative of Henry Bibb*, 169.

3. Catherine Clinton, " 'With a Whip in His Hand': Rape, Memory, and African American Women," in *History and Memory in African American Culture*, ed. Genevieve Fabre and Robert O'Meally (New York: Oxford University Press, 1994), 210.

4. *Ringwood's Afro-American Journal of Fashion*, May–June 1893, 4.

5. McLaurin, *Celia, a Slave*, 143.

6. M. A. Majors, *Noted Negro Women: Their Triumphs and Activities* (Chicago: Donohue and Henneberry, 1893), 250.

7. *Ringwood's Journal*, May–June1893, 1

8. Ibid.

9. White, *Too Heavy a Load*, 79–80.

10. "Articles of Agreement," reel 1, Records of the National Association of Colored Women's Clubs, 1895–1992.

11. Ibid.

12. *Ringwood's Journal*, May–June 1893, 2.

13. Ibid.

14. On the off chance that I have assumed a bit too much familiarity here, the names refer to Harriet Tubman, Harriet Jacobs, Sojourner Truth, Anna Julia Cooper, and Mary Church Terrell, African American women of the nineteenth century whose lives are fairly well remembered and documented.

15. See Nell I. Painter, *Sojourner Truth: A Life, a Symbol* (New York: W. W. Norton, 1996), 13, for a longer discussion of the "problem of biography" in African American history.

16. Claudia Tate, *Domestic Allegories of Political Desire: The Black Heroine's Text at the Turn of the Century* (Cambridge: Harvard University Press, 1991), does, however, offer a revealing analysis of domesticity and uplift rhetoric in novels authored by African American women at the turn of the century.

17. Lawson Andrew Scruggs, *Women of Distinction: Remarkable in Works and Invincible in Character* (Raleigh: L. A. Scruggs, 1893), 141.

18. Majors, *Noted Negro Women*, 185.

19. Coston was the pastor of Bethel African Methodist Episcopal Church at Hagerstown, Maryland, and the editor of the *Christian Reporter* for a number of years. He published *A Freeman and Yet a Slave* in 1888 while in Chatham, Ontario, as well as *Spanish-American War Volunteer*, a scathing indictment of the racism in the Ninth Infantry in Cuba, for which he served as chaplain.

20. Naming is a rich area of analysis on which relatively little work has been done. Some have argued that in cases like this, you are almost required to examine the kin networks between plantations to determine whether a group of kin had extended historical ties to a neighboring planter family whose name they carried or took upon emancipation. The name often has more to do with kinship ties to the plantation than with any special relationship with the slave-owning family. The general rules for adopting names are based on only a few studies, and while these provide creative views, they remain limited until more research is done.

21. Scruggs, *Women of Distinction*, 141. While the first issue of the magazine is not extant, Ringwood tells us in her entry for

Women of Distinction that the included biographical profile appeared in it.

22. Julia Ringwood Balch was the daughter of Susan Carter and Thomas Bloomer Balch. The white Julia Ringwood was born on Macomb Manse, Virginia, and moved to Washington, D.C., after the war, about the same time the African American Julia Ringwood and her mother did. We do not know if the sisters were in contact. Julia Ringwood (Coston) never mentions her sister, who died in 1905.

23. Thomas Bloomer Balch, *My Manse during the War: A Decade of Letters to the Rev. J. Thomas Murray, Editor of the Methodist Protestant* (Baltimore: Sherwood, 1866), 32.

24. Quoted in Majors, *Noted Negro Women,* 253.

25. Elizabeth Keckley, *Behind the Scenes: Thirty Years a Slave and Four Years in the White House* (New York: Arno Press, 1868), 38–39.

26. Quoted in Majors, *Noted Negro Women,* 253.

27. Donald G. Nieman, ed., *Black Freedom/White Violence, 1865–1900* (New York: Garland, 1994), is a good (if slightly disjointed) overview of violence directed at African Americans after the Civil War and during Reconstruction and beyond. See also Catherine Clinton, "Bloody Terrain: Freedwomen, Sexuality, and Violence during Reconstruction," *Georgia Historical Quarterly* 76 (1992): 313–332, for a gendered discussion of rape and other types of violence. I am focusing here on locales outside the South because well over 80 percent of African Americans continued to live south of the Mason-Dixon Line until well into the twentieth century. However, violence was a societal reality in the North as well.

28. The notable exceptions would of course be Harriett Jacobs's *Incidents in the Life of a Slave Girl* (1861; repr., Cambridge: Harvard University Press, 1987) and Harriet Wilson's *Our Nig; or Sketches from the Life of a Free Black* (1859; repr. New York: Vintage Books, 1983). Both document the reality of sexual terrorism and brutality and the resulting feelings of fear and insecurity on the part of the writers.

29. Nell Irvin Painter, "Soul Murder and Slavery: Toward a Fully Loaded Cost Accounting," in *U.S. History As Women's History: New Feminist Essays,* ed. Linda K. Kerber, Alice Kessler-Harris, and Kathryn Kish Sklar (Chapel Hill: University of North Carolina Press, 1991), 125–146. This work is one of a few that ask us to consider the inevitable trauma that would have been a part of slavery for African Americans. Without diminishing the role of religion and the family and kinship networks, this new scholarship argues that more attention needs to be paid to the psychological costs of enslavement. Scholars have begun to investigate the consequences of child abuse and sexual abuse on an entire society in which

beating and raping of enslaved people was neither secret nor metaphorical. Given what we know today about the effects of abuse, they ask, the way it spawns feelings of anger, low self-esteem, depression, and even self-hatred, can we discuss slavery without tackling the rage that dwelled within? As Painter points out, those who were enslaved were surrounded by and were victims of violence. They were beaten in front of their children, watched their children be beaten, and very often beat their children and each other. Painter points out that violence, rape, and incest are substantiated aspects of African American slave life. That violence, that rape, and that incest came from hands that were both black and white, hands of owner, overseer, wife, husband, father, and mother.

30. Ibid., 128.
31. Darlene Clark Hine, "Rape and the Inner Lives of Black Women in the Middle West: Preliminary Thoughts on the Culture of Dissemblance," *Signs* 14 (summer 1989): 913.
32. Jennifer DeVere Brody, *Impossible Purities: Blackness, Femininity, and Victorian Culture* (Durham: Duke University Press, 1998). Brody points out that she coined the term "mulattaroon" to denote this figure's status as an unreal, impossible ideal whose corrupted and corrupting constitution inevitably causes conflicts in narratives that attempt to promote purity.
33. Kathleen Collins, "Portraits of Slave Children," *History of Photography* 9 (July–September 1985): 187–206.
34. Quoted in Stephen Jay Gould, "Flaws in a Victorian Veil," *Natural History* 87, 6 (summer 1978), 19.
35. Ibid., 23.
36. White, *Too Heavy a Load*, 93. White goes on to suggest that the National Association of Colored Women (NACW) was so named to indicate the supremacy of a light-hued aristocracy. Of those we know to be involved with the editing and writing of *Ringwood's Journal*, a number were known to have passed for white either deliberately or by not correcting mistaken assumptions on the part of whites, among them Victoria Earle Matthews and Mary Church Terrell, both prominent in the NACW.
37. Verna Keith and Cedric Herring, "Skin Tone Stratification in the Black Community," *American Journal of Sociology* 97 (1991): 760–768. See also Bart Landry, *The New Black Middle Class* (Berkeley: University of California Press, 1987). For a full discussion of skin color and class in African American communities, see also Mary Pattillo-McCoy, *Black Picket Fences: Privilege and Peril among the Black Middle Class* (Chicago: University of Chicago Press, 1999); and E. Franklin Frazier, *Black Bourgeoisie* (New York: Free Press, 1957).
38. *Ringwood's Journal*, May–June 1893, 4.

39. Hine, "Rape and the Inner Lives," 912.
40. See White, *Too Heavy a Load*, 71–79, for a discussion of fashion in the lives of this elite group of Black women's club movement members—in particular, the role of fashion in determining the group's belief in its ability to fit into the upper-class strata of African American society and to separate itself from less educated and less economically secure African Americans.

THREE.   TO MAKE A LADY BLACK AND BID HER SING

The chapter title is based on a poem by Countee Cullen, "Yet Do I Marvel," which he ends with the line: "Yet do I marvel at such a curious thing, to make a poet black and bid him sing." I have changed it a bit here to highlight the same sort of dynamic in relation to gender ideals during the same period. The second chapter epigraph is from Elizabeth Clark Lewis, *Living in, Living Out: African American Domestics and the Great Migration* (New York: Kodansha International, 1996), 4.

1. My understanding of fashion is influenced by Crane's definition of it as "how people interpret a specific form of culture for their own purposes, one that includes strong norms about appropriate appearances at a particular point in time (otherwise know as fashion) as well as an extraordinarily rich variety of alternatives." Going beyond merely clothing, this definition encompasses the social agenda of fashion, which is at the heart of what I am attempting to accomplish in this chapter. See Diana Crane, *Fashion and Its Social Agendas: Class, Gender, and Identity in Clothing* (Chicago: University of Chicago Press, 2000), 1–67, for a fuller discussion of how this works in the nineteenth century.
2. Lewis, *Living in, Living Out*, 4.
3. Evelyn Brooks Higginbotham, *Righteous Discontent* (Cambridge: Harvard University Press, 1991).
4. Kathleen M. Torrens, "Fashion as Argument: Nineteenth-Century Dress Reform," *Argumentation and Advocacy* (fall 1999): 220.
5. Mary Church Terrell, "What the Colored Woman's League Will Do," *Ringwood's Journal*, May–June 1893, 2.
6. Ibid.
7. *Ringwood's Journal*, September–October 1893, 8.
8. *Ringwood's Journal*, May–June 1893, 2. Succeeding quotes from this issue are cited by page number in the text.
9. Jill Fields, " 'Fighting the Corsetless Evil': Shaping Corsets and Culture, 1900–1930," *Journal of Social History* (winter 1999): 128.
10. For a fuller discussion of how "divergent notions of appropriate behavior and deportment shaped the actions and interactions of elite and working-class African American women during this period," see Virginia Wolcott, *Remaking Respectability: African American Women and the Politics of Identity in Interwar Detroit*

(Chapel Hill: University of North Carolina Press, 2001), which does an impressive job of delineating the ways in which respectability as a concept underwent change and was negotiated by members of the elite and of the working class.

11. Quoted in White, *Too Heavy a Load*, 76.

12. Henry Louis Gates suggests with the phrase "representation as reconstruction" that the act of representing one's self in public, as well as in various publications, was a widely accepted strategy the elite classes of African Americans used to reconstruct and contest the stereotypical images of African Americans that circulated in nineteenth-century and early-twentieth-century popular culture. As a result of such images, African Americans would go to some lengths to show themselves as wealthy, refined, and cultured in various mediums. The ways in which the women in *Ringwood's Journal* related to these questions suggest they were very much a part of and supportive of such thinking. See Gates, "The Trope of the New Negro."

FOUR. "COLORED FACES LOOKING OUT OF FASHION PLATES. WELL!"

1. For a full discussion of Chicago's "stroll," see Shane White and Graham White, *Stylin': African American Expressive Culture from Its Beginnings to the Zoot Suit* (Ithaca: Cornell University Press, 1998), 221–247.

2. Wolcott, *Remaking Respectability*, 5–6.

3. *Half-Century Magazine*, February 1916, 46. Succeeding quotes from this publication are cited by issue and page number in the text.

4. *Who's Who in Colored America*, 3d ed. (New York: Who's Who in Colored America Corp., 1930–1932), 231. *Half-Century Magazine* would become a weekly newspaper entitled the *Chicago Bee* in 1925, and Williams would leave the magazine to take over as head of that enterprise upon its inception.

5. Daniel, *Black Journals*, 94.

6. During the first few years of the magazine's life, it focused on business and encouraged the formation of a separate Black economy. Articles informed African Americans that when they patronized Black businesses they bought jobs, entrepreneurship, and independence along with goods and services.

7. Dwight Brooks, "Consumer Markets and African American Consumer Magazines: Black America and the Culture of Consumption, 1920–1960" (Ph.D. diss., University of Iowa, 1991), 27. See also Frazier, *Black Bourgeoisie*, 34, and Johnson and Maberry, *Propaganda and Aesthetics*, 52, for a full discussion of the ways in which African American periodicals prescribed behavior for new migrants.

8. For a discussion of whiteness, femininity, and respectability in the urban United States, see Christine Stansell, *City of Women: Sex and Class in New York, 1789–1860* (New York: Knopf, 1986); Elaine S. Abelson, *When Ladies Go A-Thieving: Middle-Class Shoplifters in the Victorian Department Store* (New York: Oxford University Press, 1989); and John F. Kasson, *Rudeness and Civility: Manners in Nineteenth-Century Urban America* (New York: Hill and Wang, 1990).

9. Hazel Carby, "Policing the Black Woman's Body in an Urban Context," *Critical Inquiry* 18 (summer 1992): 739–755.

10. The Investigator, an unnamed woman, began writing an intermittent column in 1921 that chronicled what was wrong with life in Chicago. Often these investigations took on an almost undercover feel, though this one seems to have had more to do with her daily travels around the city.

11. Fannie Barrier Williams, "The Dress Burden," *National Association Notes*, Records of the National Association of Colored Women's Clubs, May 1913.

12. Ibid.

13. See White and White, *Stylin'*, 118–125, and Giddings, *When and Where I Enter*, 210, for examples of scholarly fascination with the cover of this magazine.

14. See Jones, *Labor of Love*, 163–164, for a detailed description of the numbers of African American women in various regions of the United States during this period. Another reading of the spelling of "maid" is explored in the following chapter. During this period, there was quite a bit of pressure put on young African American women to pursue domestic work as a career choice, and it is quite possible that this spelling and designation is part of that larger effort.

15. This dynamic would last far into the twentieth century. As late as 1976, researchers would discover that those in the African American middle classes put far more emphasis on the relationship between clothing and class status, while those of the professional and upper middle classes tended to believe that the connection was much less pronounced. See D. Y. Harps, "Clothing and Buying Practices of Employed Single Black Women from Three Social Classes" (Master's thesis, Virginia Polytechnic Institute and State University, 1976).

16. Valerie Grim, "From the Yazoo Mississippi Delta to the Urban Communities of the Midwest: Conversations with Rural African American Women," *Frontiers* 22 (fall 2001): 7. Grim is reportedly working on a manuscript based on a series of interviews she has done with women who migrated from the rural South to the urban North.

FIVE. NO PLACE LIKE HOME

1. Wolcott, "'Bible, Bath, and Broom,'" 88–110. See also Wolcott, *Remaking Respectability*, 1–48.
2. Catharine Beecher and Harriet Beecher Stowe, *The American Woman's Home: Or Principles of Domestic Science; Being a Guide to the Formation and Maintenance of Economical, Healthful, Beautiful, and Christian Homes* (New York: J. B. Ford, 1870), 269.
3. Marilyn Ferris Motz and Pat Browne, eds., *Making the American Home: Middle-Class Women and Domestic Material Culture, 1840–1940* (Bowling Green, Ohio: Bowling Green State University Press, 1988), 1.
4. Victoria Earle Matthews, "The Awakening of the Afro-American Woman" (1897), in *With Pen and Voice: A Critical Anthology of Nineteenth-Century African-American Women,* ed. Shirley Wilson Logan (Carbondale: Southern Illinois University Press, 1995), 151.
5. Amy Wolf, "Virtue, Housekeeping, and Domestic Space in Pauline Hopkins' Contending Forces" (1999), womenwriters.net/domesticgoddess/wolf.
6. Jane Grayson, "Gains for Losses," *Half-Century Magazine,* February 1917, 5. Succeeding quotes from this and other contemporary magazines are cited in the text, unless otherwise noted.
7. There is a Carterville in both Illinois and Missouri. It is not possible from the text to know which is meant. Since the protagonist talks of walking to Chicago at one point in the story, it is most probably Illinois.
8. Tate, *Domestic Allegories of Political Desire,* 8.
9. Booker T. Washington, "Negro Homes," *Colored American Magazine* 5 (1902): 378.
10. Edna Wheeler Wilcox, "On the Making of Homes," *Colored American Magazine* 9 (1905): 387.
11. Prof. and Mrs. J. W. Gibson, *Golden Thoughts on Chastity and Procreation Including Heredity, Prenatal Influences, Etc., Etc.: Sensible Hints and Wholesome Advice for Maiden and Young Man, Wife and Husband, Mother and Father* (Cincinnati: W. H. Ferguson, 1904), 22.
12. Wolcott, "Bible, Bath and Broom," 90.
13. Hallie Q. Brown, *Homespun Heroines and Other Women of Distinction* (Xenia, Ohio: Aldie, 1926), 212. Giddings, *When and Where I Enter,* 87, explores the relationship between domestic service and sexual violation in the Jim Crow South, and Virginia Wolcott, *Remaking Respectability,* 18, discusses the relationship of the African American women's reform movement to sexuality and the rationales for professionalizing domestic service.
14. Jones, *Labor of Love,* 156–157.

15. See *Ladies World*, July 1913, March and November 1915, December 1916.
16. Quoted in Garvey, *The Adman in the Parlor*, 143.
17. Brooks, "Consumer Markets," 77.
18. Tate, *Domestic Allegories of Political Desire*, 10.

SIX. URBAN CONFESSIONS AND TAN FANTASIES

1. *Half-Century Magazine*, February 1917, 2. Succeeding quotes from this and other contemporary magazines are cited in the text, unless otherwise noted.
2. Brooks, "Consumer Markets," 175
3. *Half-Century Magazine* (August 1916–Februry 1917). For example, "The Black Brute" (November 1916) tells the story of a white man who is masquerading as an African American in order to commit robberies and murders. An unsuspecting African American man named John is almost forced to murder one of his mistaken pursuers before the hoax is uncovered.
4. For a fuller discussion, see P. Gabrielle Foreman, ed., introduction to *Maggie Shaw Fullilove: Who Was Responsible? Stories from Half Century* (New York: G. K. Hall, 1996).
5. Brooks, "Consumer Markets," 102–103.
6. Ibid.
7. *Tan Confessions* (November 1950): 35–47.
8. After 1952, the magazine, renamed *Tan*, would more closely resemble its former Home Magazine section in content. That is to say, the "confessions" would no longer exist.
9. *Tan Confessions*, November 1950, 63. I am hesitant to say that the anonymous African American women to whom Johnson was so anxious to give authorial credit wrote the stories. While the calls for submissions told writers they could base submissions either on their lives or on stories they heard about, he also made clear that editors could make whatever changes they deemed fit.
10. All of Johnson's many magazines were based on white mainstream publications. For example, *Ebony* was based on *Life Magazine*, *Negro Digest* mimicked *Reader's Digest*, and *Tan Confessions* was based on *True Confessions*. See Ben Burns, *Nitty Gritty: A White Editor in Black Journalism* (Jackson: University Press of Mississippi, 1996); the author is Johnson's white associate editor, who discusses the color-coded mass magazine strategy John Johnson undertook.
11. Roseanne M. Mandziuk, "Confessional Discourse and Modern Desires: Power and Pleasure in *True Story* Magazine," *Critical Studies in Media Communication* 18 (June 2001): 174.
12. See Johnson's autobiography, *Succeeding against the Odds* (New York: Warner Books, 1989).

13. Johnson and Maberry, *Propaganda and Aesthetics*.
14. *Ebony,* November1955, 27–32.
15. Johnson, *Succeeding against the Odds*, 122.

SEVEN.   BUT IS IT BLACK AND FEMALE?

In the first chapter epigraph, Michelle Eubanks is quoted in Sakina P. Spruell, "As the Page Turns," *Black Enterprise,* September 2000, 95. The Oprah Winfrey quote in the second chapter epigraph is from *Adweek*, March 5, 2001, 1.

1. "Not for Women Only," *Nation's Business*, September 1994, 16.
2. "Publisher's Statement," *Essence Magazine*, May 1970, 13.
3. "Write On!" *Essence Magazine*, July 1970, 6.
4. Michelle Eubanks, quoted in Spruell, "As the Page Turns," 95.
5. Linda Peebles Pilagas, "How Latina Is *Latina?*" *Hispanic*, October 1998, 70.
6. Noreen O'Leary, "O Positive," *Adweek*, March 5, 2001, 54.
7. Ibid.

Selected Bibliography

BOOKS AND JOURNAL ARTICLES

Abelson, Elaine S. *When Ladies Go A-Thieving: Middle-Class Shoplifters in the Victorian Department Store*. New York: Oxford University Press, 1989.

Adero, Malaika. *Up South: Stories and Letters of This Century's African-American Migrations*. New York: New Press, 1993.

Balch, Thomas Bloomer. *My Manse during the War: A Decade of Letters to the Rev. J. Thomas Murray, Editor of the Methodist Protestant*. Baltimore: Sherwood, 1866.

Ballaster, Ros, Margaret Beetham, Elizabeth Frazer, and Sandra Hebron. *Women's Worlds: Ideology, Femininity, and the Woman's Magazine*. London: Macmillan, 1991.

Benstock, Shari, and Suzanne Ferriss, eds. *On Fashion*. New Brunswick: Rutgers University Press, 1994.

Blassingame, John. *Slave Testimony*. Baton Rouge: Louisiana State University Press, 1977.

Borchert, James. *Alley Life in Washington: Family, Community, Religion, and Folklife in the City, 1850–1970*. Urbana: University of Illinois Press, 1980.

Brody, Jennifer DeVere. *Impossible Purities: Blackness, Femininity, and Victorian Culture*. Durham: Duke University Press, 1998.

Brooks, Daphne. " 'The Deeds Done in My Body': Black Feminist Theory, Performance, and the Truth about Adah Isaacs Menken." In *Recovering the Black Female Body: Self-Representations by African American Women*, ed. Michael Bennett and Vanessa D. Dickerson. New Brunswick: Rutgers University Press, 2001.

Brooks, Dwight. "Consumer Markets and African American Consumer Magazines: Black America and the Culture of Consumption, 1920–1960." Ph.D. diss., University of Iowa, 1991.

Brooks-Higginbotham, Evelyn. *Righteous Discontent: The Woman's Movement in the Black Baptist Church, 1880–1920*. Cambridge: Harvard University Press, 1993.

Bullock, Penelope L. *The Afro-American Periodical Press, 1838–1909*. Baton Rouge: Louisiana State University Press, 1981.

Carby, Hazel. "Policing the Black Woman's Body in an Urban Context." *Critical Inquiry* 18 (summer 1992): 739–755.

Clinton, Catherine. "Bloody Terrain: Freedwomen, Sexuality, and Violence during Reconstruction." *Georgia Historical Quarterly* 76 (1992).

————. "'With a Whip in His Hand:' Rape, Memory, and African American Women." In *History and Memory in African American Culture*, ed. Genevieve Fabre and Robert O'Meally. New York: Oxford University Press, 1994.

Cohen, Lizabeth. *Making a New Deal: Industrial Workers in Chicago, 1919–1939*. Cambridge: Cambridge University Press, 1990.

Collins, Kathleen. "Portraits of Slave Children." *History of Photography* 9 (July–September 1985): 187–206.

Crane, Diana. *Fashion and Its Social Agendas: Class, Gender, and Identity in Clothing*. Chicago: University of Chicago Press, 2000.

Daniel, Walter. *Black Journals of the United States*. Westport, Conn.: Greenwood Press, 1982.

Fields, Jill. "'Fighting the Corsetless Evil': Shaping Corsets and Culture, 1900–1930." *Journal of Social History* (winter 1999): 126–147.

Foreman, P. Gabrielle. "The Spoken and the Silenced in *Incidents in the Life of a Slave Girl* and *Our Nig*." *Callaloo* (spring 1990): 313–324.

————, ed. *Maggie Shaw Fullilove: Who Was Responsible? Stories from Half-Century*. New York: G. K. Hall, 1996.

Frazier, E. Franklin. *Black Bourgeoisie*. New York: Free Press, 1957.

Furman, Marva J. "The Slave Narrative: Prototype of the Early Afro-American Novel." In *The Art of Slave Narrative: Original Essays in Criticism and Theory*, ed. John Sekora and Darwin Turner. Macomb: Western Illinois University, 1982.

Garvey, Ellen Gruber. *The Adman in the Parlor: Magazines and the Gendering of Consumer Culture, 1880s to 1910s*. New York: Oxford University Press, 1996.

Gates, Henry Louis. "The Trope of the New Negro and the Reconstruction of the Image of the Black." *Representations* 12 (fall 1988): 122–157.

Gibson, Prof., and Mrs. J. W. *Golden Thoughts on Chastity and Procreation Including Heredity, Prenatal Influences: Sensible Hints and Wholesome Advice for Maiden and Young Man, Wife and Husband, Mother and Father*. Cincinnati: W. H. Ferguson, 1904.

Giddings, Paula. *When and Where I Enter: The Impact of Black Women on Race and Sex in America*. New York: William Morrow, 1984.

Griffin, Farah Jasmine. *'Who Set You Flowin'?': The African American Migration Narrative*. New York: Oxford University Press, 1995.

Grim, Valerie. "From the Yazoo Mississippi Delta to the Urban Communities of the Midwest: Conversations with Rural African American Women." *Frontiers* 22 (fall 2001): 5–27.

Guy-Sheftall, Beverly. *Daughters of Sorrow: Attitudes toward Black Women, 1880–1920*. New York: Carlson, 1990.

Heermance, J. Noel. *William Wells Brown and Clotelle*. North Haven, Conn.: Archon Books, 1969.

Hendrickson, Hildi. *Clothing and Difference: Embodied Identities in Colonial and Post-Colonial Africa*. Durham: Duke University Press, 1996.

Hine, Darlene Clark. "Rape and the Inner Lives of Black Women in the Middle West: Preliminary Thoughts on the Culture of Dissemblance." *Signs* 14 (summer 1989): 912–920.

Honey, Maureen. *Bitter Fruit: African American Women in World War II*. Columbia: University of Missouri Press, 1999.

Hunter, Tera W. *To 'Joy My Freedom: Southern Black Women's Lives and Labors after the Civil War*. Cambridge: Harvard University Press, 1997.

Hutton, Frankie. *The Early Black Press in America, 1827–1860*. Westport, Conn.: Greenwood Press, 1992.

Johnson, Abby Arthur, and Ronald Maberry. *Propaganda and Aesthetics: The Literary Politics of Afro-American Magazines in the Twentieth Century*. Amherst: University of Massachusetts Press, 1979.

Johnson, John H. *Succeeding against the Odds*. New York: Warner Books, 1989.

Jones, Jacqueline. *Labor of Love, Labor of Sorrow: Black Women and Work and the Family, from Slavery to the Present*. New York: Vintage Books, 1985.

Jordan, Winthrop. *White over Black: American Attitudes toward the Negro, 1550–1812*. New York: W. W. Norton, 1968.

Kasson, John F. *Rudeness and Civility: Manners in Nineteenth-Century Urban America*. New York: Hill and Wang, 1990.

Keckley, Elizabeth. *Behind the Scenes: Thirty Years a Slave and Four Years in the White House*. New York: Arno Press, 1868.

King, Wilma. *Stolen Childhood: Slave Youth in Nineteenth-Century America*. Bloomington: Indiana University Press, 1995.

Kusmer, Kenneth. *A Ghetto Takes Shape: Black Cleveland, 1870–1930*. Urbana: University of Illinois Press, 1987.

Landry, Bart. *The New Black Middle Class*. Berkeley: University of California Press, 1987.

Lears, T. Jackson. "The Rise of American Advertising." *Wilson Quarterly* 7 (winter 1983): 156–167.

Lemann, Nicholas. *The Promised Land: The Great Black Migration and How It Changed America*. New York: Vintage Press, 1992.

Lewis, Elizabeth Clark. *Living In, Living Out: African American Domestics and the Great Migration*. New York: Kodansha International, 1996.

MacKethan, Lucinda H. "Metaphors of Mastery in the Slave Narratives." In *The Art of Slave Narrative: Original Essays in Criticism and Theory*, ed. John Sekora and Darwin Turner. Macomb: Western Illinois University Press, 1982.

Majors, M. A. *Noted Negro Women: Their Triumphs and Activities*. Chicago: Donohue and Henneberry, 1893.

Mandziuk Roseanne M. "Confessional Discourse and Modern Desires: Power and Pleasure in *True Story* Magazine." *Critical Studies in Media Communication* 18 (June 2001): 171–190.

Marchand, Roland. *Advertising the American Dream: Making Way for Modernity, 1920–1940*. Berkeley: University of California Press, 1985.

Matthews, Victoria Earle. "The Awakening of the Afro-American Woman" (1897). In *With Pen and Voice: A Critical Anthology of Nineteenth-Century African-American Women*, ed. Shirley Wilson Logan. Carbondale: Southern Illinois University Press, 1995.

McCracken, Ellen. *Decoding Women's Magazines: From Mademoiselle to Ms*. New York: St. Martin's Press, 1993.

McLaurin, Melton. *Celia, a Slave: A True Story*. New York: Avon Books, 1991.

Meier, August, and Elliott Rudwick. *From Plantation to Ghetto*. New York: Hill and Wang, 1966.

Motz, Marilyn Ferris, and Pat Browne, eds. *Making the American Home: Middle-Class Women and Domestic Material Culture, 1840–1940*. Bowling Green, Ohio: Bowling Green State University Press, 1988.

Nieman, Donald G., ed. *Black Freedom/White Violence, 1865–1900*. New York: Garland, 1994.

Ohmann, Richard. *Selling Culture: Magazines, Markets, and Class at the Turn of the Century*. New York, Verso, 1996.

Painter, Nell I. *Sojourner Truth: A Life, a Symbol*. New York: W. W. Norton, 1996.

———. "Soul Murder and Slavery: Toward a Fully Loaded Cost Accounting." In *U.S. History As Women's History: New Feminist Essays*, ed. Linda K. Kerber, Alice Kessler-Harris, and Kathryn Kish Sklar. Chapel Hill: University of North Carolina Press, 1991.

———. *Southern History across the Color Line*. Chapel Hill: University of North Carolina Press, 2002.

Pattillo-McCoy, Mary. *Black Picket Fences: Privilege and Peril among the Black Middle Class*. Chicago: University of Chicago Press, 1999.

Peiss, Kathy. *Cheap Amusements: Working Women and Leisure in Turn-of-the-Century New York*. Philadelphia: Temple University Press, 1986.

———. *Hope in a Jar: The Making of America's Beauty Culture*. New York: Metropolitan Books, 1998.

Roberts, Dorothy. *Killing the Black Body: Race, Reproduction, and the Meaning of Liberty*. New York: Pantheon Books, 1997.

Rooks, Noliwe. *Hair Raising: Beauty, Culture, and African American Women*. New Brunswick: Rutgers University Press, 1996.

Rubinstein, Ruth. *Dress Codes: Meanings and Messages in American Culture*. Boulder: Westview, 1995.

Scruggs, Lawson Andrew. *Women of Distinction: Remarkable in Works and Invincible in Character*. Raleigh: L. A. Scruggs, 1893.

Sernett, Milton C. *Bound for the Promised Land: African American Religion and the Great Migration*. Durham: Duke University Press, 1997.

Shaw, Stephanie J. *What a Woman Ought to Be and to Do: Black Professional Women Workers during the Jim Crow Era*. Chicago: University of Chicago Press, 1996.

Shevelow, Kathryn. *Women and Print Culture: The Construction of Femininity in the Early Periodical*. London: Routledge, 1989.

Stansell, Christine. *City of Women: Sex and Class in New York, 1789–1860*. New York: Knopf, 1986.

Suggs, Henry Lewis, ed. *The Black Press in the Middle West*. Westport, Conn.: Greenwood Press, 1996.

Tate, Claudia. *Domestic Allegories of Political Desire: The Black Heroine's Text at the Turn of the Century*. Cambridge: Harvard University Press, 1991.

Torrens, Kathleen M. "Fashion as Argument: Nineteenth-Century Dress Reform." *Argumentation and Advocacy* (fall 1999): 208–228.

Washington, Booker T. "Negro Homes." *Colored American Magazine* 5 (1902): 373–378.

White, Deborah Gray. *Ar'n't I a Woman? Female Slaves in the Plantation South*. New York: W. W. Norton, 1985.

————. *Too Heavy a Load: Black Women in Defense of Themselves, 1894–1994*. New York: W. W. Norton, 1999.

White, Shane, and Graham White. *Stylin': African American Expressive Culture from Its Beginnings to the Zoot Suit*. Ithaca: Cornell University Press, 1998.

Wilcox, Edna Wheeler. "On the Making of Homes." *Colored American Magazine* 9 (1905): 383–390.

Wilson, Elizabeth. *Adorned in Dreams: Fashion and Modernity*. Berkeley: University of California Press, 1985.

Wolcott, Virginia. " 'Bible, Bath, and Broom': Nannie Helen Burroughs's National Training School and African American Racial Uplift." *Journal of Women's History* (spring 1997): 88–110.

————. *Remaking Respectability: African American Women and the Politics of Identity in Interwar Detroit*. Chapel Hill: University of North Carolina Press, 2001.

NEWSPAPERS AND MAGAZINES

Crisis Magazine, April 1911.
Half-Century Magazine, 1916–1923
New York Age, June 1911.
Ringwood's Afro-American Journal of Fashion, May–June 1893,
    September–October 1893.
Tan Confessions, November 1950, December 1950.

Index

Page numbers in *italics* indicate illustrations.

About the Author

Noliwe Rooks is the associate director of African American Studies and a lecturer in history at Princeton University. She is the author of *Hair Raising: Beauty, Culture, and African American Women* (Rutgers University Press, 1996), which won a Choice Award as an Outstanding Academic Book, and the associate editor of *Paris Connections: African American Artists in Paris, 1920–1975* (Q.E.D. Press, 1992), which won an American Book Award.